WHAT OTHERS ARE SAYING ABOUT
BE THE GOOD...

Be the Good is inspiring and heartwarming but most importantly, it is actionable.

—Nir Eyal, bestselling author of *Indistractable*

When we lead with kindness and love, there's no limit to the kind of change we can make in the world. In *Be the Good*, Ken Streater cuts through the obstacles to make clear how each one of us can be a force for good every day in the communities in which we live. It's a reminder that each of us has an opportunity—and a responsibility—to focus on what's really important.

—Maggie Doyne, 2015 CNN's Hero of the Year, Co-founder and CEO, Blink Now Foundation

This short, inspiring book had me from the nuclear missile opening to the tear-jerker movie close. It offers practical wisdom on how to be a better person—and a happier one. Former river guide Ken Streater is a skillful navigator of the tricky terrain of good, and his timing is exquisite.

—Jonathan Alter, author, journalist, documentary filmmaker

Be the Good offers the wisdom of community change makers and everyday citizens from around the globe and shines light on how our world can be, where goodness abounds. Ken Streater shares powerful personal stories that show us how we each can be a greater force for good on the planet.

—Marci Shimoff, *NY Times* bestselling author of *Happy for No Reason* and *Chicken Soup for the Woman's Soul*

Now, more than ever, there is a need for people to connect with their better selves and view others and the world through the lenses of shared humanity. *Be the Good* helps us do this and act from such awareness with action steps that can easily be put into effect *right now*.

—Thupten Jinpa, Principal English Translator to the Dalai Lama, founder Compassion Institute and author of *A Fearless Heart: How the Courage to be Compassionate Can Transform Our Lives*

We've all heard about "being the change" we wish to see in the world. Now Ken Streater has given us a "how-to guide" to create that change through simple acts of kindness, compassion, and goodness. *Be the Good* invites and invokes the call to build a better world through conscious thoughts, actions, and good deeds—big or small. When it comes to the greater good, change begins within our self, our homes, and our communities, and the all is in the small.

—Barbara Edie, Amazon bestselling author of *Sparking Change Around the Globe* and *Creating the Impossible: What it takes to bring your vision to life*

With 20 practical and easy ways to become a force for good and help make the world a better place, *Be the Good* is a deeply enriching, life-changing read. In a world where we are faced with fear, famine, strife, and despicable acts, acclaimed author Ken Streater reminds us of all the good that goes unnoticed. He supports his narrative with uplifting personal experiences as well as actionable methods for us to create a positive change within ourselves and the community. The book shines a light on the simple ways each individual can create a more compassionate society by simply making strangers smile, actively focusing on the positive, learning a new skill to foster growth, and more. It is nothing short of a compelling piece of literature that will leave you changed for the better.

—Review by the Book Excellence Awards

Don't you want to help fix what's broken in society? But where to begin? Ken Streater to the rescue. He offers up an entertaining tool kit of simple everyday acts of kindness and gratitude to help us all be forces for good in our families, neighborhoods, work places, communities, and by extension the world—just when we need it the most.

—Heather Lende, NY Times bestselling author of *If You Lived Here, I'd Know Your Name* and *Find the Good*

Be the Good is an actionable guide to individual and collective well-being. It illustrates how to bring more beneficial behaviors to life in effort to build more compassionate places. With stories about his extraordinary experiences learning and working in both troubled and flourishing communities around the world, Ken Streater will inspire you to action to create a happier world promising a greater good for many.

—Dacher Keltner, Professor of Psychology and Faculty Director, Greater Good Science Center, UC Berkeley and author of *Born To Be Good* and *The Power Paradox*

Very few books in my life have stopped me in my tracks, made me put down everything I am doing, and go hug my kids. *Be the Good* got me in chapter one. Ken Streater shares his personal stories of courage, fear, trust, and vulnerability and gives us twenty simple ways to be the good and create a better world. It is a must-read!

—John O'Sullivan, bestselling author of *Changing the Game* and *Every Moment Matters*, Founder of Changing the Game Project

If these turbulent times have you scratching your head, this book may be just the salve you need. Its overarching premise is simple, yet incredibly powerful: each and every one of us can do good in the world, which in turn will make life better. The concept is made actionable through 20 specific ideas for how to actually DO good, all of which can be put into practice immediately with little to no effort. The mix of aphorisms and life advice is reinforced with a variety of stories that make it clear the author is an experienced guide on making a positive difference in the world. Being good and doing good have never been more accessible.

—Lisa Bader, author of *Wrap with Love* and CEO/Founder of Birthday Butler

BE THE
GOOD

Becoming a Force For a Better World

Ken Streater

AVIVA
PUBLISHING
New York

Be the Good: Becoming a Force for a Better World

Aviva Publishing
Lake Placid, NY
518-523-1320
www.avivapubs.com

Ken Streater
www.KenStreater.com
kenstreater@gmail.com

Every attempt has been made to source all quotes and provide
photo credit properly.

For additional copies or bulk purchases visit:
www.KenStreater.com

Editors: Nancy Gregori, Shannon O'Neill, and Mariah Wilson
Cover Design and Interior Layout: Lieve Maas, Bright Light
Graphics

Library of Congress Control Number: 2020902964
Softcover ISBN: 978-1-950241-79-8
Hardcover ISBN: 978-1-890427-30-6

Second Edition: 2020

10 9 8 7 6 5 4 3 2

Printed in the United States of America

To Danielle, Daws, Laney, and Dari

I love you.

.

CONTENTS

Introduction

Thanks for choosing to read this book. I am honored and grateful that you did. I also have a request. Will you please stop reading it after the next paragraph?

Stop and take a look around. Notice the good. It is in every direction. If you are in your home, at the office, on a plane, or sitting on a park bench, you can find positive things to watch, listen to, and feel. So, please stop reading. Take a few minutes—or more—to absorb the goodness in your world. See kids playing. Hear a friendly conversation. Feel kindness. Notice those who are doing good and those who are benefiting from it. There is a lot more goodness out there than we are led to believe. Put down the book now and see this for yourself.

(Instead of reading this, you could be: admiring a couple walking hand in hand; reflecting on your family by looking at a photo of them; appreciating someone holding the door open for a stranger; noticing a thank you, smile, or wave; or actually smelling a rose that was planted simply to make the neighborhood better. Please, close the book and take a look around. I'll wait.)

While we are told daily that the world is a screwed up place—in the harmful lessons taught by social, print, video, and news media—this is simply not true. If you just looked up and around with an open mind you may have seen a world of good. Goodness is everywhere.

These are divisive times—if we allow them to be. We don't need to conclude that someone's perspective is a reflection of faulty character or a diabolic soul, when it is simply a different perception about community or country or weather. We need not harshly label or yell at each other billions of times a day. That screeches the opportunity to see goodness to a halt.

When we see and do good things, we are changed—even if only in that moment. Our gentler nature arises. I have been fortunate to see pure goodness at work in communities from Alaska to Zimbabwe. I am humbled by and thankful for these experiences, events that triggered questions this book seeks to answer.

Isn't seeing more good and doing more good the best way to find common ground and to unite us?

How far, in terms of space, time, and lives touched, does a single act of goodness ripple out?

What if I shared good ideas by reflecting on the hope and generosity—and the fear and hunger—that I have witnessed in places near and far?

The goal of this book is to illustrate how much good is in the world and the immeasurable impact that one person can have on others. It is easy to bring more goodness to people around you, through simple acts. This book can help you identify those opportunities in your everyday life. This enables each of us individually to build more compassionate cultures. In doing so, we create societies that flourish rather than decay.

In the chapters that follow you will find twenty thoughts on creating positive individual and community change. These ideas were gleaned from experts and ordinary folk, wise elders and energetic youngsters, from humble people and heart-driven cultures across the globe. They will be valuable to you and to those around you—when you put them into action.

Many of the twenty action items in this book take very little time and can be easily accomplished. Others may take a few days or a few weeks to complete. One of the simplest ways to bring these suggestions to life is to tackle them one at a time rather than trying to adopt all of them at once. However you do it, I encourage you to let these actions become a part of your day. By doing so, you become an advocate for less fear, cynicism, and bitterness.

You help create more trusting and gracious communities. You become a force for a better world.

Bestselling author Annie Dillard said, "How we spend our days is, of course, how we spend our lives." With this in mind, the present matters more than yesterday and to-morrow. This book can empower you to positively change yourself and your community—by being the good.

1.

Be Less Certain

From the back seat of our rental car, my teenage son, Dawson, said, "Dad, did you get this message? DAD, there is a missile coming towards us." The alert then screamed on my phone: "BALLISTIC MISSILE THREAT INBOUND TO HAWAII. SEEK IMMEDIATE SHELTER. THIS IS NOT A DRILL." Since North Korea had been

Extreme Alert
BALLISTIC MISSILE
THREAT INBOUND TO
HAWAII. SEEK IMMEDI-
ATE SHELTER. THIS IS NOT
A DRILL.

launching test missiles for months—and Hawaii was one of its closest potential targets—I wondered for only a second if this was a false alarm before deciding that it could absolutely be real. I yanked on the wheel and u-turned across the highway, driving back towards the school where I had just dropped off my wife, Danielle, and eleven-year-old daughter Delaney for a gymnastics meet. We had flown to Hawaii with a few other families we knew from Central Oregon two days prior to the event. I floored it to get to the gym. As we sped back, I explained to Delaney's twin sister, Dari, who was also in the car, that we had received a message about a possible bomb headed our way, and that we were going to get Mom and Delaney, but not to worry.

I parked the car and raced towards the gym's entrance with Dawson and Dari, thinking that grabbing the other two and quickly heading north, as far away from Honolulu as possible, was the best thing to do. Many parents were scrambling around by the front door—all were stunned, some were silent, a few frantically talked on their phones, but everyone was desperate to find their loved ones. We were ten miles as the crow flies from Pearl Harbor. Surely that, or downtown Honolulu, would be North Korea's target. When we entered the gym, people were piled up in front of a small door, pushing into a tiny locker room in an effort to get deeper into the building. Hawaii residents had been practicing nuclear attack responses for the previous two months and knew what was ahead and what to do. They told us we had only twenty minutes from when the bomb was launched until it struck.

Just that morning I had told Danielle to let me handle logistics on trips like these from now on. We were going to be late for the meet because we were unorganized and had gotten a late start. Instead of arriving at 7:55, we had pulled up to the gymnasium at 8:05. This seemed like ten of the most critical minutes imaginable, to be on time for the warm up. On top of that, I was frustrated because I had to take Dari to the grocery store before the meet in order to buy two candy bars that she had promised to a friend. The two we bought the night before had been stepped on after being left on the rental condo's floor.

My concerns from earlier that morning were forgotten as I surveyed the frenzy inside the gym. As we scrambled deeper inside the building, I could not find Danielle, so I called her cell phone. She answered and said she was in the corner of the locker room. As we headed to that part of the building, a school administrator grabbed a microphone. "Folks, we have fifteen minutes until impact. All we can do is pray." With those words, we entered the tiny locker room, joining a group of about fifty people, mostly families with nine- and eleven- and fourteen-year-old children—numb and trembling.

Delaney was sitting on a bench holding hands with one of her teammates. Danielle was standing next to her. Dawson leaned against the wall, head down, and started texting his friends. Dari hugged Danielle. I scanned my phone, looking at CNN, ABC, FOX, and other major news websites for information on the attack. I looked into the eyes of other parents and saw the same helplessness that coursed through me. "What should we do?" we each asked without saying a word. "How do we save our kids?"

Dari began to cry. "Am I going to die?" she whispered. "Am I going to die?" I answered that it was going to be okay, that we were all together and not to worry. Danielle told her she was not going to die. "You promise?" Dari begged. Delaney shook as I hugged her. Dawson could only look down. I wrapped my arms around Danielle and pulled Dari into both of us.

I looked again at my phone and could find no confirmation of death headed our way. Other parents did the same, mentally demanding their devices to tell them the alert wasn't true. We all waited amid whispers, sobs, hopelessness, and love. It seemed like forever. Fifteen minutes of facing your family's death is a lifetime.

Important lessons are often painfully learned but can always lead to improvement. What I was certain mattered most as we drove to the meet earlier that morning—being late—was nothing. Nothing. The same goes for the trip to the grocery store for another candy bar. This is nothing. These thoughts crossed my mind as I weighed how impatiently and foolishly I had spent my last morning on earth, our last moments together.

Since that day, in the course of daily life, I've often asked myself how important it is to be right in any particular situation, and how certain I am about what I think I know. It isn't so much about not sweating the small stuff as it is about not letting righteousness and the small stuff in to begin with. How guilty I am of ruining far too many beautiful moments—like being mad while driving along the windward coast of Oahu on a peaceful tropical morning because being ten minutes late was unacceptable. How could I possibly believe that this was so important?

How can I look at someone I know little or nothing about and pass judgment? How can I hear a soundbite and create a strident position? How can I regard the crappy driver in the next lane as stupid? How can I preach to anyone what I am absolutely sure is the gospel truth if I don't know what is true for them? How can I need so totally to be right—again? When all is said and done, there is very, very little to be certain about, including having time tomorrow to make up for trivial pursuits founded in posturing, stereotyping, forcing beliefs, bitching about inconsequential idiocies, and being right. Certainty is itself the idiocy.

After a couple more minutes, one of the fathers said, "The alert was a mistake." He pulled up a post on Twitter from a state congressman that showed the warning should not have been issued. Others in the room began to find the same kind of news. We clung to this hope for a few more minutes, believing in the possibility that we were not actually doomed. Additional posts and reports over the next five minutes let us fully accept that a nuclear bomb was not headed our way.

Extreme stress and focusing on what to do in case of true emergencies can put a lid on emotions. As we were hit by the impact of there being no missile, the lid was blown off. Tears poured, hearts wailed, and people crumbled from sheer release. The uncertainty of any future was replaced by the seared understanding that time with those you cherish is everything.

People eased out of the locker room and into the main gym area. Strangers whispered and hugged, and coaches wrapped their arms around gymnasts and their parents. I took deep breaths and held my wife and kids, with tears streaming down my face.

The official notice of the false alarm popped up on everyone's phone, and tension ebbed into deep, deep reflection. Danielle and I sat in the bleachers with Dawson and Dari. Delaney gathered with her teammates by the balance beam. Warm Hawaiian light and easy trade wind breezes flowed across the gym floor. Or was it the collective love in our hearts mixed with sighs of relief?

I asked Dawson what he was texting when we were in the locker room. He told me that he was telling his friends goodbye and how sorry he was if he had been mean to them.

Dawson then spotted a friend at the meet and they went for a walk outside. Dari climbed a couple of rows above us to sit with her buddies. Innocent girls with fun routines ahead lined up for introductions to start the meet. Kids just wanting to be kids glowed as their team names were called, smiling from ear to ear from the excitement and aloha in the room. The mood lifted, as only it could. We all felt blessed, knowing that time is precious and love is all—and that it's best to be less certain of everything else.

2.

Share Something with Someone Who Doesn't Expect It

Give without thought of reciprocation. When you are unequivocally generous—even with one simple daily act—two or more people always benefit.

After carting mountains of rafting equipment for fifty-five hours from Seattle to Russia—in big jets, small planes, tiny cars, and rickety helicopters—the fifteen of us reached the remote river launch point in Siberia. In the late 1980s, the Soviet Union was still very much a communist country but showed signs of drifting towards democracy. Given the fledgling political shifts, a river guide friend had the idea that the time was ripe for a team-building whitewater rafting trip with both Russians and Americans. He envisioned high school students from each country running wild rivers together in the Soviet Union and the United States, as an ultimate cross-cultural, bridge-building vessel. He invited me and other guide friends to help him organize and run an exploratory scouting trip down one of the rivers intended for his youth exchange. Helping solve global political problems as a wide-eyed twenty-something in Siberia during the summer of '87 seemed like the perfect "why not?" idea, so I said yes.

Just getting to the river was a journey. It included going through Russian customs with life jackets and video cameras that put us into the espionage category and cramming rafting gear in the aisles of the regional Russian jet, because we had filled up the cargo hold with too much of our gear. Our fellow passengers, mostly residents of Barnaul, Siberia—our jumping-off point for the final overland leg to the river—were not too crazy about having suitcases in their laps for that four-hour flight from Moscow. There wasn't much cultural bridge building happening inside that plane.

The Katun River in south-central Siberia alternately meanders and rages for hundreds of miles through a seemingly endless alpine wilderness, in some of the most landlocked and isolated backcountry on earth. Azure blue and frosty cold, the Katun was home to this first expedition and several subsequent Russian and American team-building rafting trips.

A couple of days into the trip, we American rafters pulled ashore in Mul'ta to the curious stares of villagers (although to this day I am uncertain if this is the correct name of the small town). These Siberians had not seen many outsiders, let alone this type of flotilla or ragtag assemblage of foreigners. River guides often have weathered skin, bloodshot eyes, marginal teeth, a festering aroma, and questionable hair. Even better, they often stylishly complement their bedraggled aura with bright-colored life jackets. In spite of, or perhaps because of, our appearance, we walked ashore to hellos and handshakes.

After learning through our interpreter that we were the first group of Westerners ever to set foot in this neck of the Soviet woods, we were given a tour of the village. We saw hardscrabble cabins, lots of reindeer hide, a hearty group of hunter-gatherer-farmer-herder men and women, and children playing.

We discovered that what made most Soviet men and women suspicious of Americans were politically motivated stories of the "evil other side," which could include the hippy capitalists now invading this village. But, the people in this small town were largely outside of this influence. What little impact the icy government-planted tales had in this burg was easily melted away as we hung out with a couple of hundred warm souls along a remote northern river.

Within a few minutes of our arrival, we remembered the Polaroid cameras we had brought. Instant photos were cutting-edge technology in the "Oldfolkolithic" 1980s, epochs before digital anything. The people of Mul'ta only had wavy mirrors or still ponds to reflect their image. They had no photos of themselves. We snapped Polaroids and handed the artwork out amidst ear-to-ear grins and sparkling eyes. We sought nothing in return but were given joy and thanks. Our one-by-one acts of kindness brought happiness to this tribe.

We were beginning to think the Iron Curtain was actually made of chiffon when the mood grew more solemn. A teenage boy fetched the village's weapon of choice and brought it to an elder. As if to appease our respective governments that perhaps preferred us to be enemies, lines were drawn, and we faced off, with a decision made by each side to show no mercy. The same boy ran into the heart of the battlefield and held the round and worn weapon up high. At that point, we gathered around the midfield line and the skirmish began: our team of river guides against the village all-star soccer players. With little talent—on our side of the ball—and lots of laughter, we played our hearts out in a pasture arena filled with good cheer and camaraderie. It was a hard-fought game that we soundly lost.

After the game and toasts with a local curdled goat milk beverage (one of the sourest drinks on earth), with cheers all around and raised hands clutching prized photos, the village leaders bestowed on us one of their most prized possessions. The pride of our hosts was evident as they handed us one of the biggest racks any of us had ever seen—a twelve-point reindeer antler. We were overwhelmed by their generosity. And overwhelmed by our own concern, as we contemplated how to rig the five-foot by five-foot sharp-horned object on a rubber raft. We ended up strapping it to my raft's stern and fashioned a Soviet and an American flag to the antler points, all of which wisely faced away from the boat.

Generosity need not be foreign, to anyone. Whether through small acts demanding little time, energy, or money or larger ones that take a little planning, spontaneous or structured giving makes the world better, one person and one community at a time. As we bade farewell to the villagers and shoved off from Mul'ta—filled with memories and new friendships—we realized that lives are forever changed when one person or side gives to another. The idea that giving of oneself just for the sake of giving is the most powerful form of kindness washed over our group as we floated on down the river.

For years to come we returned to the Katun and discovered even more Siberian rivers and towns. On these frigid waterways, generosity paradoxically flowed, as ordinary people from mighty societies locked in heated conflict gave tiny but tremendous gifts to each other. We watched as new groups of Russian and American strangers-turned-teams rafted and grew together. During these events and through everlasting relationships born from them, contrived and supposed differences dissolved through giving. We shared what we could and grew together.

3.

LISTEN CLOSELY WHEN YOU MAKE A COMMITMENT

Notice the expectations of those around you who believe in what you are saying. This helps you keep your word.

While writing my first book, *The Gift of Courage*, I met with and learned from many purposeful people. The book tells the stories of everyday heroes who are making a world of difference in their respective communities. "Courage" is part of the title because the heroes, people I came to know and admire, were impactful in dangerous situations—and faced their own personal fears while doing so. One of them is Josh Kern, who founded and directed a charter school in one of the most violent neighborhoods on earth.

The dangers of this community—Washington, D.C.'s Ward 8—were evident every time I visited the school in the early 2000s. In a space four miles long by two miles wide and with a population of fewer than 75,000 people, 3,000 violent crimes took place every year. Most taxi drivers refused me rides to Ward 8 because they feared being robbed there.

Once, an NFL lineman-sized school security guard ushered me in off the sidewalk, afraid that I might get jumped. Street corners were framed by derelict buildings and populated by gang members. The poverty and violent pulse of this place were palpable to anyone who walked its streets. Despite this, Josh sought to change kids' beliefs about their community, themselves, and their future by opening Thurgood Marshall Academy.

As I headed to the school on one trip, I recalled a scene from *Rob Roy*, a film set in the days of Scottish kings, swords, and deadly struggles against monarchies. It tells the story of Robert Roy McGregor as he nobly fights for his community to be treated fairly by a violent and abusive royalty. He pledged his loyalty and commitment to his clan and then fought to death for it.

In one scene, Rob Roy playfully chases his kids through grasslands and spins them around in the air. They then sit on a sunlit hillside and Rob talks with his boys as his wife sits nearby.

"Father," one son asks, "Will McGregors ever be kings again?"

"All men with honor are kings, but not all kings have honor," Rob replies.

"What is honor?" asks the son.

Rob contemplates the answer. "Honor is what no man can give you and none can take away. Honor is a man's gift to himself."

"How do you know if you have it?"

"Never worry on the getting of it. It grows in you and speaks to you. All you need do is listen."

Listening matters, and never more so than listening to yourself as you offer or agree to help someone. Honor and faith are too often in short supply in our culture, despite the fact that keeping one's word is often not difficult to do (though, on occasion, it can in fact be monumentally challenging). When you do as you say, you build more trusting communities and give people more reason to believe.

I sat in Josh Kern's office one day at Thurgood Marshall Academy and watched as he juggled a million things at once: students needing to chat, secretaries asking him to call a community member, reviewing a report that needed a signature, and so on. Josh pushed and pulled and plodded through it all as I asked him questions about how a lawyer raised in an idyllic Delaware town came to be in his position.

Before Josh opened the school, he was a corporate attorney who was asked to volunteer at a local high school as part of a program for professionals to give back to their community. Josh was a guest instructor one semester at a school in Ward 8, teaching a class aptly named "Street Law," that focused on crime in Washington, D.C., and the regulations designed to deal with it. With more new metal detectors than new textbooks and a dropout rate of forty percent, Josh saw the paradox of despair and desire on display every day at this school, while other parts of D.C. flourished.

As are many of us when we see injustice, Josh was drawn to the plight—in this case, struggling teenagers who just needed a break. He knew that kids deserved a better education than they were getting. Unlike many of us, he heeded the pull to do something about it. Josh put his own comfort, honor, and faith on the line when he promised the families of D.C.'s Ward 8 that he would make a difference. As an upper-class white guy planning to call this hood his new career home, Josh made promises to a black neighborhood all too familiar with disillusionment, hardship, and pain. Once he did, he knew he had to keep his word.

After canvassing Ward 8 for a year and convincing people that he meant what he said—often in the face of disbelief and distrust—Josh opened Thurgood Marshall Academy. During the first years, classes were held in an oft-flooded neighborhood church basement and then moved to a shuttered old public school building. What started with eighty kids in a damp hole, with subsequent funds from the school district and lots of local elbow grease, soon grew to hundreds of high schoolers attending a place of hope. Josh kept his word. The result is now thousands of college-educated children leading their respective communities—in some cases, Ward 8 itself. If Josh had not followed through with his commitment, there could have been another case of dreams denied and skepticism renewed.

Josh Kern is somewhat like a modern-day Rob Roy. As the founder of Thurgood Marshall Academy, he took a broken-windowed, boarded-up building that sat on a corner of murder and mayhem and turned it into a beacon of opportunity for kids yearning for a chance. He visualized, created, and for ten years ran one of the most successful high schools in the country. While Josh was principal, every single senior at Thurgood Marshall Academy graduated and went to college. He did this with humility and grace, having once told me that he was not courageous, simply a non-conformist. "The students and the teachers are truly courageous," he said. "I just believed I could get this done and worked on it because it seemed like someone needed to."

Was it the size of the promise that kept Josh going? Could it be that smaller, everyday commitments are easier to break? Are people more inclined to keep their word when they know the impact of doing so will be significant? Why is there a lack of follow through even with the easiest of promises to keep? What impels us to do as we say or keeps us from fulfilling a pledge? Insensitivity is the most common deterrent to keeping one's word—and honor the most likely propellant.

The Rob Roys and Josh Kerns of the world—people who hold themselves accountable when they call themselves to action—keep their word, regardless of the size or impact of the promise. May we all learn from them that honoring commitments, large or small, is the most powerful way to engender our faith in one another.

4.

IN ORDER TO BE OR HAVE MORE, DO MORE

Often, doing more takes courage. How do you gain courage in order to change? Start small. Drink water, not soda. Read a book instead of watching television. Turn off the computer and go for a walk. Take incremental steps to build your courage. Little successes make bigger successes. Change creates more change. Courage begets courage.

Having a place at a dinner table set for sixteen people is meaningful in its own right. The evenings are even more special when the table is two hundred years old, the same age as the two-story, six-bedroom house it sits in on a remote Norwegian farm-turned-river-guide-compound. When the sixteen people are stoked rafting guides celebrating another great whitewater week, meaningful elevates to momentous. Dinner was a tradition for us every Sunday evening in the highlands of Norway, as we shared stories about the trips we had taken with adventurous clients in the preceding days. When this revelry is topped off by toasting a rookie guide celebrating his very first trip as a raft captain, the night turns monumental.

The guiding career of each person in the room started with a hope or a dream, like most goals that are realized. Write a book, start your own business, learn to paint, restore a classic car, become a river guide—each one of the sixteen people gathered around the table at some point in his/her life had decided to try to run rafts down wild rivers. Then they each took a small step towards that goal by being a little courageous. None went from being a college student, waitress, auto mechanic, or banker directly to the back of the raft. There was a brave little step here that led to more brave little steps there. For some guides, the initial foot forward was reading a book on river rafting instead of watching television. A few pushed their comfort zones by investing a little of their time, spending a weekend with friends who had a raft. Others took a bigger chance by signing up for a river guide school. In all cases, it was a small act of courage—not a giant leap of faith—that begot more courage, which led to steering a raft, successfully running rivers, and ultimately, after many seasons of guiding for most of us around the table, to raising a glass to Henrik, the newest member of the club.

Henrik was a young, white-collar professional from Oslo, Norway, smitten with whitewater rafting after participating in a guided trip a few years earlier. Over the next couple of years he did a few more trips as a paying client and then attended a whitewater school. To do this, he had to save money, take time off work, and commit to being submerged in ice-cold Norwegian waterways for a week in the spring. Part of his training involved swimming rapids, going into the water to learn rescue techniques, and learning how to right overturned rafts.

Norway in April is cold enough when not on a raging river. When you intentionally jump into rapids that cascade between banks covered in snow and ice, you test your courage—and question your sanity. Like all of the student guides, Henrik came through with bluer skin but was better prepared to realize his goal. After the course, for about a month, he trained on weekends in rafts captained by more experienced guides, until he was ready to take the helm.

As we sat around the big dinner table in that two-hundred-year-old house, I reflected on my path that was similar to Henrik's. In my early twenties, I was managing a sporting goods store in Southern California when my dad called to say he wanted to take my sister, brother, and me on a guided river adventure. After two days of rafting in the Sierra Nevada mountains—afraid, soaked, and never having felt so invigorated—I immediately signed up to go to a river guide school the following spring. I knew in my heart that I wanted to be a river guide. The next April, I too froze in frigid waters, learned how to steer a boat in big whitewater, and reaffirmed my desire to head down wild rivers.

I never went back to working at the sporting goods store. I guided for a few summers while going to college. After graduating, I managed a rafting company in California and spent my off-seasons running rivers around the world. Ultimately, I started Destination Wilderness, my own company that offered trips from Oregon to Idaho, Bolivia to Iceland, and Baja to Hawaii. I ran that outfit for 12 years, with up to 50 guides and myself leading global expeditions.

While in Norway, before I started my own business, I created a Norwegian whitewater school. It was during this time that I enjoyed another Sunday with Henrik and the rest of the gang. A bookish but incredibly friendly guy, Henrik stood before our group of American, Norwegian, and Danish guides and said in broken English, "Today, my dream came true." His voice cracking, hands trembling, and tears forming in his eyes—as well as in the eyes of those of us who knew this feeling and had to some degree played a role in Henrik's achievement—he looked down and then around the table at those who loved what he had achieved. He softly repeated, "Today, my dream came true. I am a rafting guide." With that he sat down, and we shouted in broken Norwegian, "Skål Henrik," and clinked our glasses to the small acts of courage—trying something different and doing a little bit more—that lead to times like this, to dreams coming true.

5.

Expand Your Innermost Compassion Circle

Those you love the most consistently get tons of goodness from you. What would happen if you grew that group, even by just one or two people?

We headed into a zero visibility storm wall. (This may be an exaggeration.) Our total line of sight was about six inches. If it hadn't been for the cockpit window, the clouds would literally have been in our face. After several minutes of blind faith at one hundred twenty miles per hour, the clouds partially parted. Dead ahead was the coast and the landing strip on the bluff. "That was intense," I said from the passenger seat of the small Cessna. "Yep," replied the bush pilot, a regular captain on this leg over Kachemak Bay between Homer and Seldovia, Alaska.

My wife and I lived in Seldovia for a couple of years while she wrote her master's thesis and I taught at the local school. This tiny town—accessible only by plane or boat—

had a total student body of ninety kids, from kindergarten through 12th grade. The pilot on this flight home was young but preternaturally calm. He had flown me many times over these waters, and I nicknamed him "The Kid" because he was just too cool. But this time his unperturbed exterior cracked after easing us down, thankful that we had not smacked head-on into another plane. "That scared the crap out of me," he said. "Hope I never have to go through that kind of soup again."

Bush flights in tiny planes and rust bucket helicopters have played a large part in my life as a wilderness guide, an Alaskan bush school teacher, and a business consultant. Whether traveling to the Yukon River delta, over high-mountain passes in Asia, or deep into African wildlands, aircraft have delivered me to micro-villages with no running water, onto river bars shared with moose, and along dirt airstrips, where children jump up and down at the sight of the plane. Once, I landed on an icy tundra runway and was shuttled to a nearby hamlet in a dogsled basket pulled by a snowmobile. As I came into town, I saw seal fur and dried fish hanging from racks next to clapboard huts. I was offered raw whale meat as a welcome package. It was very chewy.

What I realized upon my arrival, and on other journeys, is that no matter where you are, no matter how pleasant or rough the circumstances, almost without exception people have a dwelling that they treasure and depend on. A home—whether it is a five bedroom suburban house, a ramshackle cabin, or a yak-hide yurt—is the center of the universe for families. It is where love and joy and compassion most abound.

Another discovery I made on this and other sojourns is that most of us have never been forced to travel where we do not really want to go. Sure, there are work trips, funerals, and other obligations or unfortunate reasons that require us to go away from home, but even those trips are undertaken with some degree of choice or consideration. The vast, vast majority of us are not soldiers, slaves, or refugees forced aboard.

The beauty of having a home and the freedoms we enjoy made me think about places where people are uprooted by violence, death, or discrimination. My curiosity about where this most often takes place led me to Google "countries where the most refugees come from." Before I was able to click on what seemed like a relevant news article, a pop-up ad for Masterpass covered the screen. The advertiser wanted me to know about the holiday buying power of its credit card to purchase gifts for loved ones. I closed that window and found the pertinent information I was looking for—right behind the commercialism.

The article expressed what we all generally know about refugees, but it also gave a number totaling those in distress. In makeshift huts surrounded by barbed wire fences, flooded shacks on tropical forest floors, and tattered tents in isolated desert enclaves, there are fifty million refugee children in the world. Fifty million Syrian, Kurd, Afghan, Myanmarese, Ukrainian, and other children are without a country, community, or home. The value of a credit card is lost on them. They just want a home, food, and moments of joy.

Many of these children are orphans. Some have both a mom and a dad, many have only one parent, and others only an aunt, uncle, or cousin. Some have spent years in refugee camps—literal no man's lands. Others have just arrived in the camps, after treks across scorched lands, being tossed about in frozen seas, or crushed in stench-filled caravans. Each child feels hope fading or departed, but still longs for compassion.

In my search for information about refugees, I also found articles on organizations that help those that are displaced. One is The Flying Seagull Project, dedicated to bringing compassion to life and to the lives of refugee children. A troupe of clowns, magicians, and actors—most of whom are college students, retirees, or people like you and me— volunteer their time in order to make a difference. They perform, sharing dancing, music, comedy, and magic with physically and spiritually hungry kids. "We travel to camps around the world and experience the same thing every time. We have seen many kids, thousands, tens of thousands, caught up in the refugee crisis. We see tired, worn out, and scared faces. We turn those tired faces into big booming smiles," shared project founder Ash Perrin in one of the articles I read.

I didn't know Ash from Adam but wanted to learn more about his work in my quest to know and grow goodness. So I called him and asked what drove him to create The Flying Seagull Project. He answered with a question of his own. "Why is it okay," Ash wondered aloud, "that there are children in the world who are unhappy or, worse yet, so downtrodden that they are unable to even imagine?"

For the past ten years, in refugee camps from Greece to Serbia, with hearts on rolled-up sleeves, the Flying Seagulls have brought clown shows, workshops, and simple games to kids and families who are uncertain of their fate. "The feelings in the camp are stressful and dark. Hopelessness is often not a strong enough word to describe it," said Ash. "We do this not just to bring joy, but to bring reassurance. If only for a moment, a child should need not worry about anything as he or she sings or does magic or just laughs. In these moments come unconscious or subconscious realizations that things might get better, that there is love in the world for them. So, really, it is to bring love. In the face of love, children regain their confidence to express it themselves. When all is said and done, everyone wants to love."

A parent's most pressing life goal is to provide for the health and safety of his or her kids; their most instinctive need is to nurture and provide well-being in the comfort of a home. Together, these efforts help kids feel loved and happy. When these endeavors are impossible due to circumstances beyond a parent's control, it feels like the world is spinning completely out of control. "People have made this desperate decision to leave their home because they just witnessed their brother or aunt or neighbor's family blown to pieces. *They have to escape,*" explained Ash. "In some cases, they end up in places far worse than where they came from, with rows of hundreds of identical white-wall tents, unforgiving systems forced on them, not having the right to choose what clothes to wear, and with nowhere—*nowhere*—to go. They are institutionalized. Dignity is stripped away. Parents wonder if they have done the wrong thing in picking desperation and abject despondence over death. In the middle of this, we try to give families a chance to feel some normalcy. We hope to empower kids to create something, anything, and, if only for a second or a minute, to simply imagine. We allow for the dignity of being a child."

Compassion, as defined in the Compassion Cultivation Training© program, is "an awareness of suffering coupled with a willingness to do something about it." Compassion is a feeling and a desire to help. It is the emotional foundation from which springs actual walls and a roof overhead for a homeless family. From compassion comes acts of caring.

Most commonly, we are moved to compassion by those closest to us. Our family and best friends benefit from the truest gifts—kindness, laughter, comfort, time—that we share with them. Some people take this practice to a far wider level. In the case of The Flying Seagull Project, members are making it a point to bring joy and hope to people who are far, far away from their closest group of loved ones, clearly illustrating that we each have the capacity to expand our circle of compassion.

What would happen if you grew your compassion circle? Who might you notice, and what might you feel about their challenges or sufferings—and would you be willing to act on what you see and feel? Start by listing the people you love and hold most dearly, people who *have you*. Then, list five people you could care for more and would attend to if they really needed it. Pick one or two of those people and explain to them what you are doing—that you are going to be more available to help them and give more of yourself to them. Let your compassion expand and act on it now that you have made this commitment. Your gift to them is immeasurable. The gift to you is energy that begets more giving energy. This can empower you to grow your compassion circle forevermore.

The problems of the world are not too big to fix if we focus on the issues that are close to home. Decide on one or two people you can help and do more for. Then find a couple more. No tools or uniforms, like a clown suit, are needed. Just wearing your heart on your sleeve is enough to start. Imagine who you can help, and then go to them. Imagine your community and the world if everyone did this, if everyone expanded their compassion circle.

6.

Go Outside and Adventure

Get away from nonstop negative news, day and night demands, and real or imagined disasters near and far. We are made to rest and recharge, to spiritually rehydrate with nature as the elixir. This week, stand for a minute and face a sunrise or sunset, sit and rest in a field or meadow, row across a lake or on a river, head down a wilderness trail, or stroll through a park. Parched souls are best bedewed in the peace of wild places.

I remember the event more clearly than most anything else, save for the birth of my kids. Since it happened three decades ago and was one of many life experiences—and far from the craziest—I often wonder why it has stuck with me. It wasn't saving a teenager in an isolated park who had drunk himself far beyond unconsciousness. It wasn't flying in an Alaskan bush plane with zero visibility thirty feet above tundra treetops and then sliding off the end of a deep snow-covered dirt landing strip. It wasn't sitting on the banks of a remote river as a grizzly bear chased a moose towards our camp. It wasn't swerving to keep from slamming into a pickup and then careening into opposing traffic one week after my son was born. Nor was it stopping a man as he beat a woman nearly to death.

Instead, the experience in question happened as I was rowing a family of four down the Rogue River as a young-buck river guide—long before I became a father—with good times boating big whitewater as my primary life goal. The family was from San Francisco and felt a need to get away to a calmer place. We pulled ashore after making it through the most difficult rapids of the trip, in the middle of Oregon's coastal mountains, on our wild and scenic river journey. We disembarked and headed up a trail to the rustic wilderness lodge where we'd stay the night. Walking alongside me was six-year-old Danny, the youngest on the trip, who had never been on an adventure like this. He, his sister, mom, dad, and I had been in the same boat for three days, with them trusting me to get them safely down the river and back home, with hearts full of memories for life.

Danny's mom and dad were up ahead on the trail, while his sister and another guide were well behind us. As we hiked up through the forest and rounded a corner, it happened. Without a word, my young boat mate reached up and took my hand. We walked this way in silence the rest of the way to the lodge.

That was it. No cougar leaping out of a tree. No bloodcurdling scream. No slip and fall down a cliff. It was just his little hand in mine. I still feel it.

Transformation often happens at the intersection of adventure and serenity. Nature and risk-taking connect us, to ourselves and to one another. We slow down, notice things, appreciate more, and feel inspired. We discover and rediscover what matters—and each other. We recognize most of our "limitations" are self-imposed. Whether alone or with others, venturing out gives us opportunities to experience and know our place in an ecological and evolutionary continuum, which binds us as humans.

For generations we have tried to explain the importance of spending time outdoors. Even when we had more open spaces and most of our time was spent under the sun, we ventured outside for known and unknown reasons. John Muir saw time in nature as a way to "wash your spirit clean." As we became more industrialized, we continued to dare and explore. Amelia Earhart wrote, "The more one does and sees and feels, the more one is able to do." Today, getting away is even more important. Yvon Chouinard, the founder of the company Patagonia and one of the greatest outdoors-men and entrepreneurial pioneers of our time, defines real adventure as "a journey from which you may not come back alive—and certainly not as the same person."

The constant buzz and deafening hum of everyday life make it hard to experience the wonder, awe, and stillness that nature provides. You don't have to climb Everest, surf the Banzai Pipeline, or ski across the Poles to be changed. All you have to do is venture out, away from technology and the march of time, even if it's just to your own back-yard or a local park.

Humanity is essentially a million years old, but only for the last one hundred years have we dealt with exhausting rates of consumption and production—literally in the form of natural resource depletion and figuratively in terms of how tired we are from sleep deprivation and always being on the go. This means that only one one-hundredth of a per-cent (.01%) of our existence has been at this speed, in these crowds, with this noise. It is little wonder that the loudest sound we often hear is the scream in our head to get away.

So, go outside if only for a few minutes. Take someone's hand—literally or metaphorically—or maybe just take your own hand and experience reconnection. Soak up the sun, skip down a trail, and drink in the beauty of the river. Spend time in quiet open space. This may render one of the most powerful memories of your week or of your lifetime. At the very least, it will change you in that moment.

7.

TAKE CARE OF ONE PROBLEM
THAT YOU HAVE BEEN PUTTING OFF

The self-service DVD vending machine Redbox loves my wife and me. When we rent a $2.99 movie, the cleverly convenient company ends up getting somewhere between $9 and $15 because we never return our movies on time. Whether we watch the movie or not, it sits on the kitchen counter in its smug little red case for a few days more than it should. Every time she or I notice it we each get a little frustrated, often with each other: "I thought *you* were going to take the Redbox back!" Almost without fail, when one of us puts it in the car, drives it back to any one of the seven different nearby locations, and slides it into the receptacle slot, the stress goes away—and we enjoy each other's company more. With the return of the Redbox there is liberation and laughter.

So what do Redbox videos, water bills, and library books have in common? They are sources of stress for over half of the adult population in this country. The amount of angst generated when people forget to take care of what is due, and then stew on it, is the fifty-eighth leading cause of illness in America. What is the proof of this? In the Kalahari Desert or on the Mongolian Plateau and in countless other places like them, there are no Redbox related illnesses.

Truth be told, there are no statistics exhibiting that late books or overdue bills are a leading cause of illness. But it is a fact, according to the American Psychological Association, that stress is a significant factor in the six leading causes of death, which include heart attacks, cancer, and liver disease. In addition, seventy-five percent of physician office visits are for stress-related ailments.

Far too often, not dealing with stressors is perceived as easier than dealing with them. The irony here is that avoidance itself is a cause of stress—and in that avoidance the original stressor remains. The time needed to deal with troubling issues, large or small, does not just go away. When you add to this the fact that worry about stress is far more harmful than the original stress itself, you are left with a pyramid scheme of sorts that can lead to ill health, lots of time wasted in anxiety, and missed low- or no-stress opportunities.

One cost of stress is a loss of energy. Opportunities for doing more of what you want wither as angst sucks away your drive. This can keep you from doing the things that you love, like sitting peacefully in your living room, playing with kids or friends, or creating something new, like a poem, painting, scarf, blog, a healthier you, a business, or a relationship with someone who would greatly benefit from your company and wisdom. Worry about stress stymies psychic and physical energy, which are critical to creativity.

Creativity is the mother, peace of mind the father, and loving effort the grandparents of dreams coming true. With this equation in mind, by addressing and resolving something that is broken or hindering you, you give yourself more time and the tools to work towards accomplishing a goal or realizing a dream—today.

A friend of mine, Michael Neill, wrote a book about and leads seminars on creativity. He theorizes that creative energy is a ubiquitous part of the universe and is always available to us, if we let it be so. He says that this creative force commonly arises (for us to connect to and use it) in moments of enjoyment. This relationship perpetuates and grows itself. "Enjoyment leads to engagement. Engagement leads to enjoyment," he writes in *Creating the Impossible*. At the risk of revealing my firm grasp ofthe obvious, enjoyment is most often realized during stress-free moments.

At the end of his TED Talk entitled "Why Aren't We Awesomer?" Michael leaves viewers with this contemplation: You are never more than one thought away from a whole new experience of being alive. I have found this to be absolutely true (especially when I am mad at my kids) and have massaged this idea to apply to hopes and dreams coming to life. My theory is nowhere near as eloquent as Michael's, but here it is: Stressful thoughts most easily go away when you address the source of the stressor or when you recognize that it is actually just the negative thought of stress with no real stressor to be found that hinders you, which then gives you more time and energy to pursue your dreams. Anagrammatically, I call this the theory of STMEGAWYATSOTSOWYRTIIAJTNTASWNRSTB-FWTGYMTAETPYD.

Since worrying about dealing with an issue is often more stressful—and far more physically and emotionally harmful—than the actual act itself, here is my recommendation: Take two minutes to list five concerns that are causing stress in your life. Examples of these (I am personally guilty of all but one) include: an overdue conversation with someone about a challenging or troubling situation, taking your car into the shop to fix that nagging, worrisome noise, going to the doctor to check on that little weird thing on your face (instead of making your own death bed with Internet self-diagnosis sheets), paying your late water bill, or dealing with it's annoying step-sister, which is stress caused by your obsession to pay bills at least ten days before they are due.

Please write your list of concerns below. List five stressors, be they large or small. Don't fret about their order or if you are picking the right ones. That would dent the purpose of this whole chapter and make me worry about why I wrote this book in the first place! I don't need that stress.

1.

2.

3.

4.

5.

Now, pick one. Just one. Even if it is the easiest one to fix. Then take care of it, today. Stop the cycle of stress remaining or building about not addressing the issue by, you guessed it, addressing it—and by changing your thinking about it. Call the mechanic. Make the doctor's appointment. Put the payment in the mail or pay it online. Phone, email, or text the person you need to talk to or schedule a time to meet in person.

Actually, why wait until later today or tomorrow? Why not do your one thing right now? Before you read on, solve one problem. This page will automatically turn to the next page after you do.

Now that you have taken care of one issue, spend a minute recalling how much time you spent worrying about it versus the time it took you to deal with it. Notice how much lighter you feel from shedding this conscious and subconscious pressure. Then take that feeling and energy and apply it to something you want to do. Imagine how much more creative energy you would have if you readily and consistently dealt with stress-inducing issues. Regaining this energy can help you create a masterpiece, write a book, form a sculpture, plant a rose or herb garden, facilitate a community improvement project, or help others with something you are passionate about. Or you might choose to do something else, like renting an inspiring movie. Just don't take it back late. Or, if you do, don't stress about it.

8.

Whatever Your Dream, Take Your First Step Up That Path

The road to success is actually the perseverance trail. The terrain may change and the footing may be perilous at times, but walking towards your goal is infinitely more rewarding than sitting and waiting. Take the first step, then another, and then another. Along the way, take time to enjoy the views and celebrate your progress.

During the late 1800s miners risked their lives in search of gold hidden in the inland mountains and streams along Canada's Yukon River. After taking a ship to the town of Skagway, the fortune seekers would hike for days up and down snow encrusted hillsides, traversing remote mountain ridges in Southeast Alaska with blisters, broken bones, and frostbite. Death was the cost for so many during this time that the Royal Canadian Mounties began enforcing one rule in an effort to save these fortune seekers: each man on the trail had to show the Mounties that he had at least one ton of goods—food, shelter, mining tools—that would likely lead to survival and success. A ton of gear per man required multiple hauling trips and many days up and down the trail.

082921   KLONDIKE: GOLD RUSH, 1898.
redit: Rue des Archives / The Granger Collection, New York

Similar stories of hardship and perseverance unfolded in the mountains around Juneau, Alaska, just across an Inside Passage channel. Juneau sits on alluvial fans and glacial moraine flats at the bottom of fjord walls, escarpments that are backed by icefields dozens of miles wide and long. There were, and still are, no roads into Juneau. You could only arrive by boat in the 1800s. Only rutted trails and frozen cart paths ran out of town. To this day, you can't drive to Juneau, and the only roads dead end a few hundred feet or a few dozen miles from the heart of this community.

Miners hefted their worldly possessions on their backs and headed into the surrounding hills in search of gold. They set up camps in the surrounding forests. The remnants of one camp are still present a couple of miles away from the Alaska State Capitol building. But to get there, you have to hike along a steep path above Gold Creek, on the aptly named Perseverance Trail.

A couple of years ago we took a family vacation to Alaska. While my wife and kids were asleep early one morning, I went out for a hike. While standing at the start of the literal and metaphorical Perseverance Trail, I began to contemplate a goal. As I reflected on those individuals from a generation long removed—who had committed life and limb to building a better life—I took my first steps towards changing how I fit into my industry. Relatively speaking, my goal was far less arduous than theirs but it would also require some commitment and gumption. After years of loathing my role in the ego-driven, profit-oriented, and relatively heartless commercial real estate brokerage profession, I stood at the edge of an Alaskan rainforest wishing that my life were different. I dreamed of being proud of my work, my company, and who I was, instead of being emotionally divorced from my job and foreign to myself.

Before real estate, I had spent two decades as an international adventure guide and outfitter, leading expeditions to life-changing destinations, where heart and soul led—like a beautiful mountain trail—to wonderment and peace of mind. Along the way, I got advice from a mentor to use income from my business to invest in real estate that was needed for the outfitting operation. Instead of paying rent to someone else for a guide house or equipment warehouse, pay it to yourself, he said. He added that most likely no one would value my business as much as I do when it comes time to sell it and retire, but I could realize income from the real estate I own.

As a new father concerned with the wellbeing of my kids, I took this to heart. I worried about leaving them with nothing and about whether or not outfitting would ever be financially secure enough to raise a family. I bought a couple of small properties and noticed that I liked the process. My office manager at the time predicted I would be a real estate broker, but I discounted that idea, believing the lifestyle rewards from guiding and outfitting could never be replaced with that line of work. But, she was right. I sold my outfitting business and got my real estate license and went to work as a broker.

The next few years, I felt like I was trudging along with two-thousand pounds on my shoulders, wasting time, skills, and desires on work I deemed unfulfilling and lacking honor. From this frustration and my memories of life-changing experiences of rafting clients in my prior work, I visualized making a difference by introducing sweeping changes in the real estate industry to humanize it and make it more rewarding for all concerned. But this dream always ended up seeming too daunting to undertake—until I stood at the start of the Perseverance Trail. It dawned on me that those pioneers of the 1800s took one step at a time to get where they were going. In some cases they had to reverse course and pick up cached supplies to meet the Mounties' mandate. They did this, and then headed deeper into the mountains, ultimately reaching their goal.

So, I needed to rethink my course. Maybe even backtrack. I decided that when I got back to my desk, I would share my vision with everyone I worked with. I had to start vocalizing my belief that success at the expense of another person or one's community was not true success. I told clients and brokers who had closed off parts of themselves in the singular pursuit of money that I did not want to do business this way. In some cases, I lost business. In other instances, clients were refreshed by my honesty and commitment. While there were some people who tried to knock me off this course, I refueled by reminding myself of this needed shift in societal priorities, and kept on moving.

As I hiked the Perseverance Trail, I also promised myself that I would take steps to publish articles, write books, and speak about leading with one's heart. By doing so, I attracted like-minded clients and colleagues, who also put community before commodity, pursuing the greater good over profit at any cost. "Just business" in our office became a phrase that meant fair and ethical practices rather than excuses for bypassing doing the right thing. With the vision, aid, and support of my brokerage co-owner and our crew, we are making headway towards reforming the commercial real estate culture.

Taking that first step allowed me to create new ways of doing business. I used a trowel rather than a bulldozer to start forging a trail that ended up in a gold mine, where doing right by others superseded making money at any cost.

There are still no roads to anywhere from Juneau, much less a road to success, but it was here that I realized dreams come true along a perseverance trail. Rather than waiting for a road to be built, just start hiking. Take your first step on the path to wherever you want to be.

9.

TRAIN YOUR EYES TO SEE THE GOOD

What you see is what you look for, so try and change what you notice. Notice cloudscapes instead of the frustrated drivers when you are stuck in traffic. Watch as the door is held open for someone while you wait in line at the bank. Catch people smiling at each other. Your heart will be glad you did.

Cornsilk. Peru. Papayawhip. Burlywood. Oldlace. I can't say with one hundred percent certainty, but I think the only thing these words have in common is that they are names of colors used in website design. While there are over sixteen million different color combinations available to use on computer screens—with names weird and normal—some lucky but very unusual people can recognize a billion different colors in any real world scene. Research tells us that most people are capable of seeing a million to seven million unique colors at any given moment, whether staring up a quiet Colorado country road or glaring up a congested California freeway. Up to seven million choices! That is a lot to choose from.

I was once stuck in a taxi with three friends for over four hours in a Soviet city of about a million people. The car was a Russian version of a Geo Metro. That's not a lot of space for five people. The driver spoke no English and we spoke no Russian, unless you count bread, please, thank you, big, and grandma (babushka). At first, we looked longingly out of the car windows at one ashen streetscape after another, searching for the apartment of a new Soviet friend, the address of which had been illegibly scribbled on a matchbook cover.

About an hour into the impromptu tour, my comrades and I actively decided to change our perspective. We started to notice all of the good things about the city. We spent the rest of our time marveling at the hardiness and amenities of the place and laughed at our predicament rather than growing increasingly frustrated. Our time in the minnow car turned into a colorful adventure, including the colorful language (we believe) of the wayward cabman, who eventually found the apartment building.

We have millions of choices of colors in life to notice, but far too often we focus on the grays. If given the choice between sea green, light salmon, goldenrod, or dim gray, which color would you prefer to see? Take time right now to run these colors through your mind. Mentally picture each one. For a few seconds, give yourself the gift of a rainbow brain.

Now, take it a step further. If you had the opportunity to witness sadness or happiness, sorrow or joy, or pain or pleasure, which would you focus on? Ask yourself this question honestly, and then test it today at work, driving to the grocery store, working out, or watching television. What are you choosing to see?

We are each blessed with the Reticular Activating System (RAS), which is a brain function that helps prompt and filter what we observe. Originally "designed" to help assure survival (e.g., catching a hairy beast out of the corner of your eye because your brain told your vision to be on the lookout for hairy beasts), the RAS today gives us the ability to look for what we want to see.

Psychologists call a form of this Confirmation Bias. This simply means that we interpret what we see based on existing beliefs or a desired outcome. In other words, preconceived notions literally and metaphorically color what you observe. If you are on the lookout for your friend's red SUV, you will notice more red cars. If you are searching for a file on your computer, you will see similarly named files as you scan your screen. What you see is what you look for.

Given this knowledge, why not change what your look for? See that yellows make you feel warm. Observe that greens give you more hope. Notice lilac to relax. Look at the blue sky ahead instead of the bumper in front of you. Focus on tulips instead of traffic. Find a smile instead of a frown. Train your eyes to see the good.

10.

Make a Stranger Smile, Today

My friend and cofounder of gud vyb, Mitch Rost, and I were on a flight home to Redmond, Oregon, after a business meeting in Southern California. In the late 1990s, my wife, Danielle, and I moved to Central Oregon from Alaska because we wanted a place to base our growing outfitting business that offered trips in Oregon, Idaho, Alaska, and Northern California. Our goal was to find a beautiful area with a small-town feel. Plus, Danielle is a city girl turned country mama who loves to ride horses, so having some open space mattered. We found an ideal spot on the eastern base of Central Oregon's Cascade Mountains. After driving around the Northwest for a couple of weeks, we discovered that the people of Central Oregon were exceedingly nice. It was a no-brainer to settle down here.

Mitch's kids and my kids go to the same school. We became friends, and Mitch and I spend a lot of time together coaching our daughters' sports teams, working out, participating in the Warrior Dash and other athletic competitions, and talking about community. He is a physical therapist by trade, an inventor by avocation, and a philanthropist by nature. We often contemplate how to spread kindness but spend much more time laughing at and with each other. gud vyb is a result of those conversations and laughter. We created the gud vyb app in order to make it easier to say thanks and acknowledge goodness that people bring to the world. Actually, he invented the app; I am riding in the tailwind of his genius.

This particular flight home from Southern California happened before we had firmly landed on the gud vyb concept, but the conversation we had on that flight was integral to the project. We were deep in conversation about making the world better—or maybe just discussing the texture of our shoelaces—when we decided to create a list of ways people could make each other feel better or at least make someone else smile. At the top of the list of how to share good vibes was simply to smile at someone in hopes that they would smile back. We have all done this, given a quick smile and a nod to someone who gives you a polite response in kind. However, research indicates that receiving a genuine smile can improve happiness and increase faith in others, while quick, insincere grins can engender a lack of trust. With this in mind, we concluded that if brief smiles did not guarantee a positive heart-felt response, then maybe something that took more time might.

After debating the amount of time it would take to inspire a genuine smile in another person, we decided to experiment. Our back-of-the-napkin reasoning led us to believe that if you could smile non-stop at nothing in particular for twenty seconds that you would: (1) look like a weirdo, (2) make the person who was watching you smile, or (3) both. So we tried it on each other. I had an aisle seat on the plane and Mitch was sitting by the window. The middle seat was unoccupied, which to this day we regard as a blessing for whoever would have been there. After four rounds of rock-paper-scissors to determine who went first, I sat with a smile on my face, looking around and at Mitch for around twelve seconds. He quickly broke and cracked up. Then he went. About nine seconds into his happy-go-lucky grin, I smiled from ear to ear.

We decided to experiment more widely with our twenty seconds theory. Our plane landed in Seattle, and we headed to the food court during our layover. After burritos—and several minutes into our test—we were likely regarded by our hungry fellow travelers as two very strange dudes or recent lottery winners. I would smile off into space for twenty seconds while Mitch scanned the crowd to see if anyone smiled at my smiling. A couple of people did, but most looked away, hoping not to make eye contact with the bizarro before them. Then Mitch would go. Same response. It was fun just smiling away, but we realized that this tactic was not the best way to get a stranger to smile or make someone feel better. We did, however, find quantifiable and repeatedly verifiable evidence that people eating at the next table would find another place to sit.

People more mentally stable probably would have packed it in at this point. But we didn't. Instead, we came up with better ideas, which we crafted into a simple list of how to inspire strangers to smile and how to bring more joy into people's lives. We encourage you to try one or all of them, or to create your own list. We also encourage you to take the next minute to smile for twenty seconds.

1. Buy a small bouquet of flowers at the grocery store and give it to the checker.
2. Pay for the coffee of the person behind you in line.
3. Leave change in a vending machine.
4. Let the person behind you at the grocery store go in front of you regardless of how much is in his or her cart or basket.

5. Send your spouse, partner, or a friend flowers at work for no reason.

6. Write out your favorite positive quote and give it to someone who would find it meaningful.

7. Give someone a small packet of herb seeds that they can plant, even in a window box.

8. Write a friend a note of admiration and appreciation and put it under his or her windshield wiper.

9. Send dessert to a table of strangers.

10. Give someone a check for five dollars with the request that they fill in the blank "pay to the order of" line with their favorite charity, and then mail it in.

11. Make or buy two lunches and give one away.

12. Compliment someone in front of others.

13. Tell your favorite joke to someone at work.

14. Give a kid a fist bump or high five.

15. Add a candy bar to your groceries at the check-out stand and give it to the person behind you as you finish checking out.

16. Give a friend a box of herbal tea.

17. Order pizza to be randomly delivered to your co-workers.

18. Say "way to go" to someone running by on a trail or at the gym.

19. Notice something good about the next person you see and say so to him or her.

20. Dance to no music in front of a group of people. (OK, never mind. Mitch and I will handle this one.)

11.

Remember What You Have Accomplished

When we remind ourselves that we have dealt well with many challenges in the past, we feel better about the chances of overcoming more challenges in the future. Remembering and saluting what you have successfully faced gives you more strength to get through another difficult task.

Let's make this idea interactive. I encourage you to write down five things you have effectively handled or overcome in your life. Raised kids? Check. Fought through a serious illness? Write it down. Worked your way up a career ladder in spite of missing rungs? Give yourself credit. Rebounded from a broken heart? Record that.

At one point in my life, I spent twenty or more hours a day for eight straight months lying in bed or on the floor. I had ruptured a couple of disks in my back from years of bodily abuse as a river guide and then disregarding early warning signs to take care of my lower back. The result was stabbing nerve pain down my right leg that prevented me from standing or sitting for more than a few minutes at a time. It felt like a freight train was running back and forth over my leg. My days consisted of making myself something to eat, going to the bathroom, taking half-a-block walks, and looking at the ceiling fan. As a thirty-something, I was distraught by the belief that this would be my life, forever. Until, gradually, I got better. Now I use this period as a reminder of what is possible even when you feel like there is no point in trying or going on. I also know that this challenge pales in comparison to what far too many others in the world have to endure in the form of severe physical challenges or deep emotional scars.

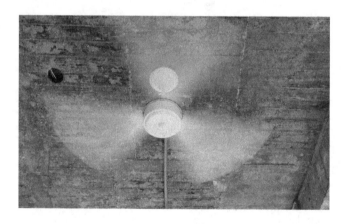

Simply put, you and I and others have overcome challenges that could have sent us spinning down, down, down—never to get back up. But we got back up. The problem is we often forget just how talented, resilient, focused, determined, and capable we are. And we most often forget this when we need it the most—when we need to pull it together, find another way, and lift ourselves up off the mat: when we need to elevate.

If you have not written down your list of five things, please do it now.

1.

2.

3.

4.

5.

Thanks. Now, take out your phone and snap a photo of this list. The next time you are wondering if you are going to make it, if another step looks to be one too many to take, look at this list. Carry it with you to hold in your heart, to honor all that you have been through, and to remember the gift that it is to you now. This reflection will change your perspective about what you face today. It is your past overcomings—and the reminder of the strengths that you have—that form your ability to rise above or push through the next challenges you will face.

12.

ACT WITH HEART AND WITH HEARTS IN MIND

Always remember that there will be someone up or down the line who is to some degree hurt or healed by what you do. Each action you take will at some point affect someone's heart.

My morning commute is a study in values. When I take my twin daughters to elementary school it seems like all of the drivers are cautious and kind while dropping off their kids. People's cargo is precious around a school. We drive with our hearts wide open—and in the back seat. Even drivers traveling through the school zone without kids ease it back, probably sensing the affection in the air—or they are afraid of getting a speeding ticket. This atmosphere and the school zone speed limit law are both born of love and consideration. We don't want to hurt our kids.

Once we're back out on the highway away from the school, things change. Maybe it's because we are late for an appointment. Maybe we don't want to go where we are headed. Maybe it's because we just watched our baby head up the school steps, away from us for another day. Whatever the reason, we often switch from caring to glaring, stuffing our hearts away. Determined driver brains and fully fueled egos take over. School zone cool is replaced by hot steam.

I've noticed that the same thing happens in business. As a fifty-percent owner of a commercial real estate firm that facilitates well over one hundred million dollars in transactions a year, I witness fascinating behavior when clients sell or buy investment properties. In this pursuit, hearts are not always engaged or even in the same room. Far too often, they aren't even in the building. I've observed that people who are compassionately cool in the driver's seat as they drop their kids off at school in the morning—revealing a full capacity to act with their heart and other's hearts in mind—get steaming mad while seated at the negotiation table.

This paradox crystallized for me one day on the Oregon Coast, before I was a partner in my current business. On a rainy spring day, my wife, children, some of their friends and I walked down to the beach. At the ocean's edge, the kids were running around, getting wet, looking for shells, throwing sticks, and jumping over creeks. They were laughing, and my wife and I were smiling. Then, my cell phone rang.

It was the broker representing a multi-millionaire seller of a twelve-million-dollar property that my Fortune 500 client was buying. A disagreement over the sale terms was getting nasty and needed to be hammered out. My client wanted the seller to provide a fifty-thousand-dollar credit at closing for a piece of building equipment that needed to be replaced. The broker, whom I had known and liked for many years, and I had been cordial up to that point but now things were heating up. Neither side wanted to give in. So, while my kids played in the mist with their soaked rain jackets and innocent spirits keeping their hearts warm, I started yelling at the broker. And he yelled back.

We metaphorically stood toe-to-toe, arguing over what amounted to less than one half of one percent of the deal. Now, don't get me wrong, fifty thousand dollars is a lot of money, and my fee for facilitating this transaction was sizable. But what is it worth to turn away from the beauty of your family and sour the sweetness of the moments around you? After hanging up the phone, I felt like an ass for yelling at someone. As I let my boiling blood reduced to a simmer, and returned to the joy at hand, I wondered—as I have wondered for years since—why can't we shift away from archaic head-to-head business mentalities and engage in heart-to-heart relationships, whether in front of a school on Main Street or inside of a high-rise on Wall Street? After this argument, I vowed to make this ideal a reality.

In preparation for starting our real estate business, my partner Andrea "Andie" Edmonds and I referred to three books to form our foundation: *Start with Why* by Simon Sinek, *Delivering Happiness* by Tony Hsieh, and *Born to Be Good* by Dacher Keltner. We read other books and attended several personal and business development seminars. We looked deeply into the holistic aspects of entrepreneurship and social responsibilities therein. The retreats and readings asked questions of our hearts and suggested that what matters most in business is doing what you know to be right—and helping people find happiness. We recognized that right really doesn't need to be analyzed, that we all intuitively know what right is. Excuses or justifications come from ego or greed. Right comes from the heart. We concluded that potentially every transaction would at some point affect someone's heart, as with most interactions in life.

Today, our brokerage operates with the immovable ideal that community comes before commodity. In other words, with every deal we examine the value of the transaction to the community rather than solely on the financial return on investment, whether it is a warehouse, office building, retail center, or apartment building. We wonder if a deal will bring quality jobs to town. We ask if it serves a portion of our population that needs vital services, like affordable housing or occupational training. We examine if the money made by the investment will be reinvested in a socially responsible way. We study whether our ecosystem will be made better.

Community

At the heart of a successful transaction is a basic human connection. Whether your needs are in Central Oregon or across the country, we strive to build relationships within the community by collaborating with local experts. Put simply, we believe in Community before commodity.

"They are more passionate about what they do. More caring. They want you to have the best option for you. There were many times they went out of their way to help us."

Honesty

We believe Honesty should be an inherent attribute of any relationship, but too often we hear stories where it is absent and trust is violated. While it is easy to throw out buzz-words, we invite you to talk with our clients and hear their expe...

began to think maybe we could do ..
things ...

We also believe that each broker has far more important things to do in life than just make money. We created an environment that supports family as our first fortune, where no one is required to be in at a certain time and stay for a prescribed number of hours. The only quota question we ask is "are you happy, fair, and professional?" We have turned the phrase "just business" on its head by working with honorable clients as opposed to those who justify unethical behavior strictly in the name of profit.

As we implemented these practices, we discovered that most people agreed with them. We found that bankers, title company officers, insurance agents, tenants, investors, real estate brokerages, and others appreciated a community and compassion-first approach. We found that many of our existing clients shared the same philosophies but had been hesitant to publicly express them or had not found the appropriate partner to embolden their social consciousness in business dealings. New clients liked what they heard and selected our firm because we took these approaches. And brokers wanting to make a bigger difference in their community came on board. We found that heart belongs in business matters. Our brokerage grew four hundred percent in three years.

Recently, Andie and I held our annual goal-setting meeting with each of our brokers. While asked in different ways, the primary question for each person was "Are you fulfilled—on all levels?" One of our brokers, Rachel, struggled with her answer. She told the story of a client who had made an offer on an apartment building and wanted to remove all of the tenants so he could fix the place up and charge a lot more rent. While on the one hand it made sense to improve the quality of the apartments, Rachel shared with us how this meant that four of the occupants—elderly residents on fixed incomes—would no longer be able to afford living there or any other place in town. Their rent would increase by two hundred and fifty dollars a month or more, which they couldn't afford.

Realizing that the financial return on his investment was paramount to this buyer, we did the math at the conference room table. We discovered that instead of a six and one-half percent return rate on his investment by kicking people out, should he elect to continue renting to the four seniors at their current rent rates his return would be almost exactly the same, even after he fixed up their apartments. Together, Rachel, Andie, and I figured out what Rachel might say to her client that would illustrate the concept of hearts being affected by his choice. Rachel said that she would speak with him about the small financial difference as well as the big heart difference. By doing so, she would draw attention to the fact that with any action we can either harm or help someone down the line. Ultimately, this client decided not to buy the property for a couple of reasons, one of which might have been examining the deal not only from a financial perspective, but with his heart engaged as well.

After this meeting, I headed to my daughters' elementary school to pick them up. As I drove, I could have sworn that people were more polite than normal on the highway. At the school, many of us parents, grandparents, and babysitters gathered as always just inside the playground fence. For some reason, the usual friendly conversations seemed even more animated and meaningful.

As kids spilled out of their classrooms, I wondered if this was the normal afternoon drive and playground tenor. As they ran across the school grounds toward us, I realized the work my team and I had done had brightened the day, lifted my spirits, and was going to have a positive impact on my daughters' hearts.

13.

GO DISCOVERING, WITHOUT A DESTINATION

To see more, hear more, and know more, do more. Go dancing, visit a museum, try a new sport, read lots of books, join a special interest club, or take someone who inspires you to lunch. Growth is fostered through discovery.

Leading physical and mental health experts say that dancing with a partner is one of the best activities for better health. According to Dr. Patricia T. Alpert, the founding dean of nursing at Arizona College and the former head of the physiologic department at the University of Nevada, Las Vegas, dancing leads to better balance, memory boosts, increased flexibility, cardiovascular efficiency, muscle strengthening, diminished depression, stress reduction, weight loss, and enhanced interpersonal relationships.

There are tons of dance choices. Competitive tango is one. Another is line dancing at your favorite country bar (the gains of which might be offset by drinking too much beer, which could be counter-offset by the good feelings you get listening to songs about driving your truck up country roads with your loved one and your dog settin' next to you). A third might be the arms akimbo limbo at your next reggae party. Regardless of which you choose, dancing is good for you.

The number one tango dancing country in the world is Argentina, which is logical since the dance originated there in the late 1800s. The second most tango-happy country is... Finland. Other than Argentina, more people per capita do the tango in Finland than in any other place on earth. Finland also consistently ranks as one of the happiest and healthiest countries in which to live. It turns out that cold winter nights heated up by spicy salsa sashays equals a high quality of life.

But there is more to it than dancing. Revealing statistics are found in television viewing, literacy, activity participation, and education studies. Finland is always ranked as one of the top countries for the least amount of time its citizens spend watching television. Americans spend over twice as much time watching television as the Finns. In addition, Finnish people are the most literate people on earth. Their heritage encourages reading—not news media watching or Internet use—as the best form of information gathering and resource for creative thinking. This comes as the result of a homogenous culture that long ago formed habits like reading as a way to pass the time. Finns have developed a deeply entrenched belief in having full access to knowledge, in large part because they "believe in the power of reading to foster well-being," according to Dr. Iris Schwanck, director of the Finnish Literature Exchange.

Finland is also the most physically active country in Europe. Ninety percent of its populace participates in hour long or more fitness activities at least twice a week. On a per capita basis, no country has won more gold medals at modern Olympics than Finland. For years, Finland has also won the crown for the world's best public education school systems.

After my second trip to the Soviet Union, I overnighted in Helsinki. The colors of the city—the blues, pinks, greens, and yellows of buildings, the eruptions of flowers, the boats in the harbor, the clothing—stood in stark contrast against the coal- and fog-shaded life of Moscow. Helsinki felt *alive*. I saw this on every corner. Perhaps Finnish citizens do a lot with their lives because of their recognition that freedom is precious, a knowledge born of sharing a border with a totalitarian society.

Some naysayers opine that Finland's education system is better than others because it is not a very populated country. But this argument is countered by Finland's even less populated neighbor, Norway, which ranks sixth in the world in education (and which the Norwegians have every right to be proud of!). There are telling reasons why Finland has achieved such success. Finnish students don't start school until they are seven years old, elementary and middle schoolers don't have homework, and there is only one standardized test required during their entire educational career, when students are sixteen years old. Students are encouraged in and out of the classroom to discover more—about themselves and the world around them. They aren't required to learn in order to perform well on a test that illustrates where they rank in a narrow band of criteria. They aren't asked to do rote exercises every afternoon and evening but instead are given hours a day to explore what they like, how they fit in, and who they are.

Experience can come from innovative education systems, participating in activities, reading, or just not watching as much television. We are healthier when we come to know more about ourselves and those around us—through experience. We are better when we understand and engage with others in our communities. We are happier when we take time to go dancing or just explore and share what we discover.

Look for more to see, hear, know, and do. Discovery leads to growth. Growth leads to a better life.

14.

SPEND MORE TIME IN THE COMPANY OF HEART-DRIVEN GENIUS

Concerts, book readings, plays, sporting events, and other live shows are events brimming with energy. As artists and athletes share their genius, with honed gifts that come from their heart and soul, we are lifted up. The vibrations at live events are contagious and bonds are formed. When we tap into this collective spirit, we learn how to build more cohesive communities.

At a recent concert, my wife and I and a couple of friends laughed our guts out, sang at the top of our lungs, and danced like maniacs. We also silently listened to the slower songs, in a mellow sea of people held in an old rocker's sway.

A couple of weeks after that gig, I took my thirteen-year-old son and his friend to see an indie surf punk rock band. We had been to shows as a family, but this was his first concert for just him and his favorite kind of music. He pressed against the stage and moshed with the best of them. I sat above the fray in the balcony, feeling like I belonged in a rickety wooden rocker rather than being one myself. I rallied through three hours of the loudest music ever, grateful for two earplugs plus a wad of toilet paper in each ear as I watched my son and his friend jamming. The entire place—except for the balcony—was a roaring sea of kowabunga crowd surfers.

In 2016, the U.S. music industry capped a record growth year that saw gross revenues exceeding seventeen billion dollars. Of this money, nearly fifty percent was spent on live music events. Broadway shows had their greatest income year ever as well, with a five and one-half percent increase over the previous year. Nearly one and one-half billion dollars was spent by people wanting to experience shows put on by some of the most brilliant live performance actors on earth.

Musicians, actors, authors, athletes, and others who share their genius move us beyond ourselves. Passion on stage creates an atmosphere of reverence and rapt attention. Witnessing heart-driven talent helps us recognize our own unique capacity for purposeful achievement. Soulful sounds and soliloquies soothe us. We revel in the gift of genius and greatness. Sharing this with ten or ten thousand strangers unites us in these moments and in memories forever. The proof of this lies in the enduring power of Woodstock and Lollapaloozas—passed into our culture along with the goosebumps we get when we reflect on concerts we have attended.

Americans spent eight billion dollars on concerts in 2017, doubling what they spent ten years earlier. Why do we spend so much to go to live events? Why is this number growing so dramatically? We go to concerts and plays and book readings to be entertained. We go to spend time with family and friends. We go to be touched by others. We go to escape. We go to have fun. We go to *unlayer*, as artists open their hearts and we open ours. We go to be awed by what humans are capable of.

Our daily lives are too often consumed by shoulds, have-tos and worry-abouts. We spend a lot of time just going, and often not enough time going in the right direction. Social media and technology may connect us electronically, but they isolate us physically. We don't regularly slow down enough to examine and salute our individual greatness and collective potential. We are systematically separated by speed and stress. So we go to shows to be with other people who also want to both get away and come together.

Live events are energy shifters, issuing a vibrational pull that sends us to another place. This place is where we are united and reunited by common chords. These are the times when we go all in—and all in as one. This group spirit is a reminder that we can lift ourselves up when we coexist in the sway of each person's heart-driven gifts.

15.

COMMUNICATE YOUR POSITIVE THOUGHTS

Sharing such thoughts out loud brightens two worlds.

For a few years when my kids were younger, I'd end the bedtime routine every night with a positive comment about each of them. I would share something I saw each one of them do or some quality of theirs that impressed me. As I tucked them in, I would share my appreciation. "I loved how you laughed with your friend when you walked to the car after school." "It was great that you did all of your homework on time tonight." "You are working so hard at your soccer dribbling and it shows." "How did you get so cute?" I believed they would fall asleep with these positive thoughts. Who knows if they did? It might be they fell asleep thinking about their teacher or friends or sports cars or soccer cleats or clouds.

As I write this, I can't figure out why I stopped saying these things each night. I am going to restart expressing their goodness to them.

I have coached youth sports for a decade. I started with soccer when my son was five years old, and I have coached my girls' teams for six years. At every practice and every game I tell every player at least one thing he or she did well. Of course, I also share my perspectives on what they can do better. When I see a player do something impressive, I say what I thought about it. It makes the players happy and they try harder. And it makes me feel good that they feel good.

After doing this for a couple of seasons I noticed how often outside of the youth sports arena that I would think something positive about someone but not share that thought with them. When I paused to think about it, I wondered what was stopping me. Then I noticed that others didn't do it either. You can see in someone's face when they are impressed with someone in their company. You also notice that this positive impression is rarely expressed in that moment. This seemed ludicrous to me.

We have over fifty thousand thoughts a day. Most of them are habitual and repeated, over and over and over. According to numerous psychology studies, roughly eighty percent of our thoughts are negative. Positive thoughts are relatively rare. Why not do what we can to tip that balance?

Now, when I have a positive impression of someone, I share it. By telling them, texting them, or emailing them, I tell them my thought. I just say it. It makes them feel good and it makes me feel good. And that qualitative rationale doesn't even take into consideration the quantitative mathematical side of this equation. Because when you share a positive thought you have about someone, you are spending less time thinking negatively and more time with positive thoughts—and others are spending more time with positive thoughts too, about themselves and about you.

Let's tip the thought scale. Let's brighten the world. Just say it when a positive thought crosses your mind about some- one. It's a sound idea.

16.

Slow Down

Soothe your mind by doing something you love, working on a simple project, or just taking a few deep breaths. Camp next to a river or in a mountain meadow. Put a jigsaw puzzle together. Fly a kite. Play tennis. Star gaze. Crochet. Walk. Good ideas happen and deeper connections between us are made when thoughts unclutter and slow down.

In the days following the most recent presidential election, I watched my kids play with their friend who came to our home for a sleepover. My wife and a friend went out for a drink. And my buddy Brian and I worked out together and sensibly talked about Republicans and Democrats and the state of the States. All the while, my mind spun at what this election meant.

My children's friend is from a family whose parents and grandparents voted for Trump. My wife's friend voted for Trump. Brian did not vote for Clinton or Trump. My wife and I voted for Clinton. By the time you have read this you likely have already decided something about everyone I've just mentioned above. I assume this because I suffer from this same affliction—when my mind races, I race to conclusions.

My guess is that after reading the paragraphs above your thoughts did not sound like, "It is great that kids are having fun in a comfortable home." You probably did not think, "We are fortunate to live in a place where two people can safely go out to talk and laugh over glasses of wine." Maybe after reading about Brian you thought he did not fulfill his free-world duty, or maybe you didn't blame him for not voting for either one. I wonder if you noticed that two friends helped make each other better by exercising together or that we were trying to make the world better by talking about it. Odds are, like me, you focused on a narrow portion of the person you got a glimpse of and, like me, could not understand how someone could possibly have voted that way.

The week after the election my good friend and musician Joe Fred emailed me a *Head and the Heart* cover song he had just recorded to soothe his mind. The lyrics include:

"I can get lost in the music for hours, honey, I can get lost in a room.
I can play music for hours and hours, but the sun will still be comin' up soon.
When the world is spinning a little too fast, it will slow down for we are meant to last.
So just for a moment, let's be still. Just for a moment, let's be still."

So, here's an idea. Be more still.

I remember rowing a raft a few years back on the wild and scenic Rogue River in Oregon. On the second night of this late fall trip, a storm packing ninety-mile-per-hour winds and horizontal rain blew through our camp. Tents were knocked over and one-hundred-year-old towering pine trees snapped all around us. We hurried to the camp kitchen in the middle of the night to put all of the gear on the ground and cover it with tarps and rocks so it wouldn't blow away.

In pitch blackness we returned to the few tents that remained standing and tried to go back to sleep. It was impossible. Five-thousand-pound trees shattering all around you leaves you with only two things to do: close your eyes and hope for the best. There was no escaping this maelstrom. There was nowhere to go to get out of the darkest of nights and craziest of storms. I lay awake, tossing and turning in my thoughts, believing that my world could be coming to an end, crashing down all around me.

Morning broke with lots of good news. All the camp gear was still there, no one had been crushed, and the sun rolled in behind the mist. My river friends and I were safe and glad to be alive. *We were glad to be alive.* Because I had an appointment the next day, I had to leave my friends after breakfast. They were going to take their time floating the rest of the river and spend another night. I headed down-river in my raft, all by myself. As I rowed through a narrow stretch all I could hear was the sound of the oar blades breaking the river's surface and the canyon wall rivulets whispering into the river. The peace completely contrasted with the powerful devastation of the night before. And even with a couple of rapids coming up around the corner, just for this moment, all was still.

I have never lost a job as a steelworker or a coal miner. I have never been treated differently because I was black. I have never known the challenges of being a single parent. But I have been desperately in debt and out of work. I have been surrounded by gangs that wanted to beat the crap out of me because I am white and they are black (that and the reverse were what happened where I grew up). I was raised by a single mom who juggled life alone. There are times when my mind spins out of control with worry about things, some I can control and others that I can't. I place blame, I get angry with others, and I wonder how we got into this social discord mess. But, when I quiet my thoughts, compassion takes hold. When I soothe my mind, I can actually feel what someone else might be feeling and respond accordingly.

It's possible that we have reached a breaking point. We did as a union just before the Civil War. We did as a country when the civil rights movement and the Vietnam War tore us apart. While violently painful and scarring, we came through these events and many more like them, not unscathed but maybe a little more understanding. Now slavery is regarded as inhumane, soldiers are no longer spit on when they return home from war, and women of all colors peacefully march in the name of social justice. We took a collective deep breath and took stock of the good things we have. We still have a long way to go, but by calming ourselves down we can focus on what we have in common, and make deeper connections.

Rivers have a way of turning out calm. Rapids can toss and turn over a raft, but below every rapid is a stretch of quiet water. Storms can rile up a waterway until it is unrunnable, but then the storm passes. Time and distance on a river mean that you will end up moving peacefully to your destination. A journey down a river is made up of this: old and new friends who marvel at what we all see and feel—the beauty of where we are and the comfort of good company.

Some people choose to gaze at the stars and others prefer to study them, but each of us likes the idea of a better life. Before saying another word, before trying to figure it all out, let's just drift a bit. You find something to do that brings you peace, and I will do the same. As we do this individually, why not sit in awe at the same goodness that surrounds us all. Let's slow down, be more still and connect on this level.

17.

Talk to Someone New

Make a list of three people you know, but not very well, who have very different perspectives from yours about religion, politics, music, or something else you value. Take one of them to lunch or out for coffee. Just talk about life. Look for what you share. It is likely you will find a lot in common.

ru gonna tmb or do ig? check out my gr8 post on fb*

Instagram, **Snap**chat, and **Tweet**. Notice how the rate of speed and the speed of time are reflected in the names of today's leading communication apps. We have created delivery mechanisms and an abbreviated language to instantly broadcast our thoughts. However, the leading platforms now recognize that it may take more than a couple of words or lines to share something important. Some now support the idea that it is worthwhile to take more time to communicate.

For years, you could use only a hundred and forty characters on Twitter to share wants, needs, ideas, good news, bad news, displeasure, amazement, or happiness. Twitter now allows subscribers to use up to two hundred and eighty characters to express their thoughts. Said Twitter on this expansive occasion:

> "Our research shows us that the character limit is a major cause of frustration for people tweeting in English. When people don't have to cram their thoughts into 140 characters and actually have some to spare, we see more people Tweeting—which is awesome!"

The above tweet is a hefty two hundred and fifty-nine characters.

Twitter, Snapchat, Facebook, Instagram and others can be very helpful platforms. They allow us to easily share happy and sad events in our lives. They provide a palette of opportunities to post ideas that move us. They simplify and magnify how family and friends keep in contact. Social media has made communication quick and easy. We can touch more people in less time than ever before.

But speed has a downside. Rapid-fire soundbites that are immediately interpreted by others impede a deeper understanding of issues—and of one another. Fairly deciding if someone or something is okay, worth getting to know, promote, embrace, share, or erase is virtually impossible based on a meme, a post, or a two hundred and eighty character tweet. Meaningful decisions and solid relationships are not made quickly and easily within character limits. Quality time spent with others remains the cornerstone of real connections. These connections— not links born of opinion bursts—remain the key to better communities.

In their eye-opening study on the power of spoken versus written words, researchers Nicholas Epley (a professor of behavioral science), Michael Kardas (a Ph.D. student at the University of Chicago), and Juliana Schroeder (assistant business and psychology professor at U.C. Berkeley) concluded that spoken word conversations may "enable partisans to recognize a difference in beliefs between two minds without denigrating the minds of the opposition." They found that face-to-face interactions—not social media posts—more clearly illustrate what is on someone's mind. They also discovered that "hearing a person explain his or her beliefs makes the person seem more mentally capable." This means that we are far more open, impressed by, and sensitive to others—especially those with whom we may not agree—when we communicate in person.

When was the last time you spent a couple of hours just visiting with someone you don't know well? When was the last time you intentionally spent an hour in the company of someone you believe is very different from you? By contrast, how much time do you spend on social media?

At the corporate and organizational workshops I facilitate, we ask participants to list three people who are very important to them or who have made a great impact on their lives. These can be people they know personally or have never met. Often, it is a friend, parent, sibling, entertainer, religious figure, business leader, or community member that they list. After they come up with the three, they are asked to list three characteristics that these three people share. Doing this exercise helps people discover the interpersonal traits that most matter to them. Then it gets even more interesting.

When people in the room say these traits out loud, the actual number of different characteristics is very, very small. Almost without fail, you can count the number of interpersonal values we all highly regard on fewer than ten fingers, with the most common including compassion, integrity, kindness, and bravery. When someone from the left side of the room realizes that a person from the metaphorical right side of the room has the same ideals—and that certain values are universal—they meet in the middle around these traits. People on "opposite" ends of political, social, religious, and other spectra discover that they are far more alike than not. This very well may be the case with someone you believe to be very different from you.

An expressed goal of this book is to create more caring communities. You have the ability and power to make this happen. Make a list of three people you believe hold opposing values from yours. Invite one of those people out to lunch or coffee. Ask him or her to tell you about one of their favorite people, and to share that person's most meaningful characteristics. Then, share your important person and his or her traits. At the end of your time together, make a plan to meet again, take a selfie of the two of you, and share it on your favorite social media account, along with a few words about what you have in common. It'll make a gr8 post on ig or FB.

* Are you going to tweet me back? Or can we talk on Instagram? Check out my great post on Facebook.

18.

BUILD AN EMPOWERMENT TREASURE CHEST

Pick three songs, three quotes, three videos, three books, and three friends that inspire you. Create an electronic folder on your personal device or computer to house these items. Label it something fun like "My Do-More Dossier," "Growth Spurt," or "Motivational Dream Machine." When you need a pick-me-up, a different perspective, or a shot of self-confidence, go to your folder and read, listen, call someone, or watch something that gives you fresh energy. This emotional and mental boost will lift your spirits, help you metaphorically travel to a better place, and refill your tank with can-do fuel.

As a contributing editor to the website *motivation.com*, I am a student of how and why people create goals—and what they do to meet them. *Motivation.com* is dedicated to helping people achieve success as they define it, and offers articles, videos, and dialog on how to do this. Over the years, I have read book after book on the psychology of motivation and spent time in the company of leading personal development experts, largely in an effort to figure out how we can lift ourselves individually in order to lift ourselves collectively.

I have also watched and analyzed more empowerment videos than should be legally allowed. Scenes from the movies *Rocky*, *Rudy*, and *Remember the Titans* are apparently required for any video to be considered a legitimate YouTube inspirational. Songs by Queen, Pink, Ed Sheeran, Madonna, and Survivor are the requisite background music for these videos.

I walk around a lot these days with my arms above my head, fists pumping, while loudly humming "Eye of the Tiger." Truth be told, I am not a hundred percent sure of how loud I am, as ambient sound-canceling, extra-bass headphones fill my cranium with that boom-boom-boom. When I get to the chorus, I am so into it that I start singing out loud and my outstretched whirligig hands actually touch the sky. I find this routine helps me get what I seek, like a table in my favorite restaurant. People in a Denny's lobby tend to scurry from a singing shadow boxer waiting to be seated. Without fail, I am immediately escorted to my favorite back corner booth and given endless free appetizers. The only thing I don't like about this is that it is hard to sing out loud with a mouth full of mozzarella sticks. You don't suppose that is why they keep them coming?

Countless goal-setting studies have been undertaken to discover why some people get and stay motivated and

why others don't. No research I'm aware of has found a single magic pill, one guru to follow, the best affirmation to repeat, and, despite my best efforts to gain superhuman strength from singing the lyric "it's the eye of the tiger, it's the thrill of the fight," no specific song that readily and repeatedly peps people up. The one single tool that will help everyone realize dreams doesn't seem to exist.

What we at *motivation.com* did find in academic studies and anecdotal evidence is a reminder that even the most diligent among us can overlook the obvious. We discovered that attaching your deepest emotions to goals is vital to dreams coming true. Whether the love for a child, ecstasy of achievement, or joy of living your strengths and passions, it is tugging heartstrings that keep people focused and driven.

Personal growth for the sake of the individual is valuable in itself, but greater good takes place when self-improvement positively impacts communities. The formula looks like this: Empowerment is the gateway to people flourishing, and when people flourish greater good manifests. Put more succinctly and in a way that Einstein might have found legit, $E+F=G^2$.

In examining how an achievement formula could best work for individuals, communities, and the world over, we figured out what everyone needs to grow and succeed: an empowerment treasure chest. Turning to a propelling resource when things get tough or an obtacle appears is invaluable. So, here is our suggestion: Starting now, list three songs, find three quotes, come up with three meaningful videos, download three inspiring books, round up three photos of your favorite people or places, and write down the names of three people you know who lift you up. Then, literally create a file on your device with these items, aids that are designed to *touch you*, to pull on your heartstrings when you need a tug.

Don't worry if the things and people you choose aren't "perfect" or that you can't find every single item. You will likely add some things and swap others out over time. Trying to make it perfect right off the bat is detrimental rather than helpful. Just fill your chest as best you can. Your choices should bring a tear to your eye, a smile to your face, and a flush through your heart. If they do, they are good empowerment treasures. When a song inspires you to sing out loud, a video makes you cry, and a passage or perfect word shivers you in awe, you are connecting to what matters. In these moments, your goals are given life. For all of the benefits that your accomplishments give to us, fill your chest today.

19.

CREATE AND CARRY
A GOODNESS TOOLKIT

Pack extra compliments, easy-to-do good deeds, plenty of positive cheer, hands to help people up, and a smile. When you carry and use it every day, you make the world a better place.

When my daughter Delaney was seven, the two of us watched the sun as it tucked itself in for the night, settling down behind the Three Sisters Mountains—named Faith, Hope, and Charity. Its work was done for now in our part of the world. Delaney and I stood quietly together with our own thoughts. Maybe she was reflecting on the day, the sunset, or life in general. "Happy makes me happy," she said.

Happy makes us happy. Sadness makes us sad. Harshness makes us harsh. Kindness makes us kind. Goodness makes us good. With this in mind, in addition to carrying a purse, briefcase, cell phone, the weight of the day, and precious memories like the one above, why not carry a goodness toolkit? It weighs little and is worth far more than its weight in gold.

A couple of years after that sunset, I walked into our kitchen one afternoon where my kids had created an impromptu diner. The sign on the playroom easel for their establishment said, "Welcome to the Hooray Café!" They made me a sandwich. As I ate, we chatted about their day. Their good deed diner lifted my spirits.

I thought, "Why not take this concept further?" Could there be a better place where you can go to get, give, and feel good, receive good news, good ideas, good stories, and a chance to hear about and do good deeds? So we created *hooraycafe.com*, a virtual version of that "diner." Hooray Café now shares good news stories from around the world and has launched the Goodness' Sake Project (GSP), an initiative to grow positive acts and sentiment in towns, companies, and organizations around the world.

The GSP is a goodness toolkit for communities that we have unveiled in a couple of towns. It offers devices and programs that make it easier to spread compliments, generate good deeds, facilitate live fundraising events, and create caring committees to lift communities up through generosity. Generosity is relatively simple and can be immediately impactful. For example, last night when my daughter and I went into a sandwich shop, the two guys in front of us were waiting for their meat to get microwaved. They generously asked if we wanted to go in front of them. We were touched by this gesture and, even though they did not expect anything in return, when we paid our tab we asked the cashier to apply our change to their bill. We walked out and thanked them without telling them what we had done, confident that as they had with us, we lifted their spirits.

The Goodness' Sake Project was initiated to provide more positive news content for Hooray Café. We figured this was a way to make more good news, one place at a time. Through this project, communities will be able to empower their citizens to do and be more for their compadres. Countless medical studies and sociologic research projects have found that doing good for others and randomly giving of your self improves physical health, mental and emotional wellbeing, workplace and recreational performance, and interpersonal connectivity. With this in mind, there is no reason to wait until GSP comes to your town to help create a better vibe for you and those around you. You can implement your own "spirit lifting devices" right now.

Here are a few items to put into your goodness toolkit:

1. **Compliments:** Find something you like or admire in a "perfect" stranger, and tell them what that is. In other words, just pay someone a compliment. For example, "You look great in that shirt" or "I love your smile."

2. **Deeds:** Do more simple good deeds. As part of the GSP project, we created "Do Good Now" boxes and placed them in coffee shops, book stores, gyms, and other retail locations in select communities. Patrons are invited to pull a random card from the box and do what it says. There are thirty different cards that spell out ways to do spontaneous good deeds.

   You don't need a "Do Good Now" box to do a good deed. Why not do these today? Put your hand on someone's shoulder and tell them "Thanks for being _____ (you fill in the blank with one of their positive attributes)"; without being asked, offer to babysit for a friend so he/she/they can go out, and; early in the morning, send someone a link to an inspiring song. Tell them that the song reminds you of them. By doing this, their day will start out on a very positive note.

3. **Thank you notes:** Leave a note on the computer, desk, or windshield of someone you appreciate. This does not have to be a calculated production. When a thought about someone's goodness crosses your mind, put it into writing and make sure they get it.

The GSP provides magnets that can be left on cars of people who are appreciated. We call them "You Matter Magnets," and they say things like "Your kindness is a gift to our community," "Our community is richer with you in it," and "People like you inspire people like me." Use one of these phrases or write whatever you feel and leave an anonymous note where your friend, co-worker, teacher, boss, employee, or community member can find it. Why anonymous? Because the recipient will contemplate the positive impact they have on a variety of people if they don't know who the note is from.

4. **Good vibes:** Send good vibes, of love or gratitude. The "gud vyb" app is one way to do this. By blending technology with kindness, gud vyb makes it quick and simple to share tokens of appreciation. The app enables and inspires people to send messages or emails of admiration and thankfulness to friends, clients, community members or deserving strangers. It is a fun and easy way to compliment someone for any number of reasons.

The gud vyb app was created because we need more good vibes. We need to balance the slew of less positive information that continuously comes our way. "Vybing" someone—saluting kindness, acknowledging effort, expressing love—takes only seconds. Your gud vyb to someone can instantly shift energy up, to a level that brings more good.

5. **Smiles:** Smile more often.

In his book *Man's Search for Meaning*, holocaust survivor Viktor Frankl states that "happiness cannot be pursued; it must ensue, and it only does so as the unintended side effect of one's personal dedication to a cause greater than oneself . . ." A recent study undertaken at Switzerland's University of Zurich discovered that the parts of the brain associated with happiness consistently fired when participants gave or thought about giving. This means that there is scientific evidence to support Frankl's idea, and then some: Happiness ensues from giving. From this, as declared by an old-soul seven-year-old during a sunset, happy can make you even happier.

20.

CHOOSE TRUST OVER FEAR

After 30-plus seasons coaching my kids' various sports teams, I was ready to hang up my whistle. I had coached or helped coach soccer, basketball, and football every fall, winter, and spring for ten years. I loved guiding young athletes but felt I had little to offer as they grew older, since I lacked deep expertise in any of these sports. I knew young adolescents deserved more sophisticated instruction in order to advance their game. But my eleven-year-old twin daughters and their friends talked me into coaching one more soccer season.

A couple years ago, and several months before my last coaching gig, one daughter gave me a note to read as I left for Grand Forks, North Dakota, to give a speech. When I committed to this event I had no way of knowing that it would be on the same weekend as our town's annual Daddy-Daughter Dance. We had gone to this winter ball every year since the girls were six years old. In her note, Dari said how sad she was that we would not be able to go to the dance together, but also told me she was excited as she knew how much this presentation I would be giving meant. In a couple of spots on the note it looked like tear drops had smudged the ink, which broke my heart. In spite of her pain, at the end of the note she wrote, "I wish you lots of luck, and lots of hope."

The folks in Grand Forks were reeling from an act of violence at a local coffee shop. The recent Somalian immigrants who owned it had seemingly melded into the town, and yet they were the targets of a right-winger's firebomb. Their business and building were destroyed. Immediately after the fire the family decided to not reopen their shop out of fear, as tensions over migrants had reached a boiling point. This normally cooperative community was struggling with its identity.

I reached out to the TEDx Grand Forks organizing committee to express my interest in talking about the importance of choosing trust over fear in a community—especially after events like the one they just went through. They invited me to come speak. In front of a welcoming audience, I shared stories of my world travels where I had witnessed the best and worst of humanity. I knew of towns and countries that had been hampered or destroyed by fear and other places that flourished in trust. I provided ideas for Grand Forks to find ways to mend, by moving forward with a heritage of trust that had long held this community together. I ended my speech with Dari's note in my hand, reading her last line and relating that trusting places breed hope, which leads to dreams that manifest into reality. When a collection of good dreams come true, individuals and communities thrive. This is what I wished for Grand Forks.

I went home and returned to the soccer pitch for one last season. What I lack in technical knowledge I have always tried to make up for with tons of positive support and camaraderie building. Every season, I urged boys and girls to play with strong legs, clear heads, and full hearts in order to do their best for themselves and for their team. I was ready to try this one last time, although I was worried that I was burned out and might have trouble keeping my head clear and my heart full. Then, onto the practice field walked Ashlee. She had never played a game of soccer in her life, but was willing to give it a try.

Ashlee and her sister had been raised in a neglectful home. Their mom struggled as a single parent and was unable to provide for them. The dad was nowhere around. Ashlee's grandparents, who had long since raised their own family, took the girls in. But the sisters had grown fearful of people. Their trust in anything was virtually nonexistent.

The root of the word trust is Old Nordic "traust," which means "to make someone feel safe and strong by allowing them to rely on your integrity." The word first appeared about a thousand years ago. Considering that our early ancestors initially roamed the earth millions of years ago and some form of spoken language has been around for sixty thousand years, verbalizing the idea of trust is relatively young. But the concept is not.

In his landmark book *The Third Side*, Harvard professor William Ury examines prehistoric, ancient, and modern-day cultures to ascertain how long competition for resources, the use of violence for power, and the idea that we need to fear one another has been around. His anthropological studies revealed that ninety-nine percent of our human timeline has essentially been free from fear of one another. In other words, only for one percent of our existence has trust been trampled on. Based on genetics and the obvious everyday desire among most people to trust others, having fear be a guiding force in life is troubling. So much so that it leaves one's heart far from full, like Ashlee's.

At first, Ashlee would not sit in the circle we formed before and after practices to talk about our hopes, challenges, and successes. She would sit just outside the ring of teammates. At other times she would kick the ball as hard as she could away from the rest of the team and then slowly walk to retrieve it. And sometimes she would walk as others ran laps. Her actions told me that she wanted to show us that she didn't need or trust us, that she would be just fine on her own. At this point in the season, I did not know Ashlee's story, but I knew she was uncertain and hurting.

Over the next several weeks, we gave reasons for Ashlee to trust the team. After every practice, I gave her and each player a big hug and told them how impressed I was with something they did. Her teammates made room and asked Ashlee to sit in the circle. I demanded that she run laps with the rest of the team. Her fellow players cheered her on. Ashlee's grandfather high-fived her after every practice. Her wary look turned into an occasional smile that became an ear-to-ear grin, as twice a week for practice and once a week for games Ashlee's heart was gently held by those around her. She found a place where she could feel safe and strong. She was given a chance to choose trust over fear.

Ashlee's grandparents made sure she came to every practice and cheered her on at every game. She was almost always the first player to arrive and one of the last to leave. She learned to practice hard and compete harder. By the end of the season, Ashlee was a leader on the team. She was our best goalie and one of our top scorers. She believed in her new family, her coach, and her teammates. Despite a short life of more sorrow than joy, more despair than hope, and more suspicion than faith, she came to believe in the possible—and in others.

One idea I shared with the folks in Grand Forks was to give of yourself in a way that those around you knew that you had their best interests at heart. I also suggested always being dependable. And I laid out how trust can be built or rebuilt by simply listening to each other. I encourage audience members to put all of this together and to act on what they learned and knew to be right.

After the show, attendees warmly shared with me their stories, hopes, and projects. One person spoke of the food co-op he helped create that engendered trust and collaboration across age and economic strata. Another spoke of her successful yoga practice that served residents of a traditional farm town who trusted the young entrepreneur because she clearly illustrated that she had their best interests at heart. A third shared how the Somalian family that owned the café in town was overwhelmed by how people listened to and expressed regret over their tragedy. Ultimately, the owners of the restaurant decided to move to another small Midwestern town because relatives there needed help with their restaurant, graciously declining the financial and hands-on support extended to them by the people of Grand Forks.

I had seen these types of efforts in action around the world and was heartened by how folks in the audience were using the same ideas to improve their community. I headed home full of gratitude, awestruck by the resilience and kindness of the town and the power of trust that was rebuilding Grand Forks. I was equally humbled when I got home and saw more of the same on our small-town soccer field.

Becoming trustworthy—trust worthy—doesn't take much. It is first making a decision to allow trust to be a guiding life principle. This happens most easily when you witness and absorb the goodness in your community instead of overreacting to those who do not have your best interests at heart. When people you initially feel may not be interested in giving or receiving trust cross your path, instead of finding them flawed, consider exploring what you have in common. And discover what is really troubling them. Odds are it is not you and it is not a lack of deep desire to trust. While it might take a few minutes or a day or two, giving them time is far better than adding fuel to their distrust fire by ridiculing or dismissing them. Then, you are really showing that you care. This enables you to build hope in others, one person or one soccer player at a time. It empowers you and others to discover or rediscover trust and give more people a reason to believe in its power.

If a wounded eleven-year-old girl who had every reason to fear can find a way to trust, then so can you and I. Let's build places of hope. Let's choose trust over fear.

Afterword...and Forward

Last weekend our family watched the movie *Wonder*, based on the novel by R.J. Palacio. August Pullman is a fictional boy born with many physical challenges, including a horribly disfigured face. His disfigurement made him feel like a freak so he had stayed at home most of his early life. "Auggie" suffered through months of bullying and pain during his fifth-grade year—his first at an actual school as he was homeschooled up until that point. His parents knew that he needed to find comfort and confidence out in the world despite the abuse he might first have to endure, so they enrolled him in school.

Initially, kids shunned and made fun of Auggie. Then, he made a couple of new friends who sat at his lunch table and worked on school projects with him. These kids defended Auggie when he was picked on. They showed other students that he was a warm-hearted kid worthy of kindness. Gradually, he came to be admired by many other students.

My wife and I pretty much cried through the entire movie. We were reminded of the beauty of love that helps a child persevere and thrive, the senselessness of bigotry and ridicule anywhere and at any time, and how kinship and happiness ensue from generosity. Ultimately, we were again left with the idea that doing good matters and matters and matters more.

Towards the end of the movie, Auggie and his classmates sat in the school auditorium for the graduation ceremony. From the stage, the principal quoted Henry Ward Beecher: "Greatness lies, not in being strong, but in the right using of strength; and strength is not used rightly when it serves only to carry a man above his fellows for his own solitary glory." The principal continued as he prepared to announce the surprise winner of the "Beecher Award," the biggest of the day. This honor historically went to the most notable student, based on volunteerism and school service—the one that gave and meant the most to others. "He is the greatest whose strength carries up the most hearts by the attraction of his own." With that, the principal announced August Pullman as the winner. Auggie walked on stage to the raucous applause and affection of the entire school.

I wrote this book with my shortcomings, loves, struggles, and dreams exposed. I wrote it with my heart on my sleeve. I have shared these contemplations for a variety of reasons, not the least of which is to relearn them myself—and for my kids to have a better place to live. In the middle of this writing, we were in Hawaii for the terrifying missile alert and once again experienced how fleeting and precious life is. This reinforced my desire to share these ideas in order to make our world better.

I don't apply what I suggest as often as I'd like, but I keep trying because I have seen these lessons work around the world. I have witnessed their effectiveness in lifting communities, one person at a time. I hope you give these ideas a try and forward their intent, for your benefit and for ours. You and I can make the world better. I encourage you to feel the rewards of fostering more goodness. I invite you to carry up the most hearts by the affection and attraction of your own.

ABOUT THE AUTHOR

Ken Streater is a former international river guide, Alaskan bush schoolteacher turned social-good entrepreneur, Fortune 500 consultant, speaker, and author. Even with a couple of college degrees and a handful of businesses that operated around the world, most of the ideas Ken shares arise from chance encounters in threadbare or thriving faraway places.

As part of his wanderings and global work, Ken has been involved in many one-of-a-kind and eye-opening experiences. They range from praying for his life in a miniscule dugout canoe as territorial mama hippos snorted threats to squash him to trying to protect his family from a nuclear missile attack; from being one of the first Westerners ever to set foot in a middle-of-nowhere Siberian hamlet, aptly named Reindeer Hunting Village, to strolling among and showing support to stunned protestors on the streets of Hong Kong during the Tiananmen Square uprising; from participating in scary and sublime first rafting descents on remote rivers in North America, Europe, and South America to creating a company that facilitates approximately $150,000,000 a year in real estate transactions.

Ken's writing helps individuals, communities, and businesses change their beliefs and behaviors in order for their homes, towns, and workplaces to become more humane. His multifarious shared experiences foster an awareness of the fundamental importance of the common good. His stories provide actionable guidance for each of us on how to elevate society to a higher standard, where compassion, collaboration, and healthy sustenance undo and supplant shortsighted, damaging ways of life.

Ken is the author of *The Gift of Courage: Stories of Open Hearts, Kindness, and Community* and his upcoming book, *The Art of the Heal*. To find out more about these book and other projects, including select readings and other live events, please visit www.kenstreater.com.

To take a survey on your desire and ability to be a community, business, or global change maker, please visit www.kenstreater.com/changemaker.

PHOTO CREDITS

Page 15: Dawson Streater

Page 19: Danielle Streater

Page 21: Danielle Streater

Page 25: Indigo Brude/Suzanne Canja

Page 26: Indigo Brude/Suzanne Canja

Page 28: Indigo Brude/Suzanne Canja

Page 32: Car Ballou, Getty Images/Istockphoto

Page 34: Stephen Voss

Page 36: Stephen Voss

Page 40: Grethe Hostaker

Page 41: Ine Skjorten

Page 43: Tomorca, Getty Images/Istockphoto

Page 46: Glenna Alderson

Page 48: Djenkaphoto, Getty Images, Istockphoto

Page 49: The Flying Seagull Project

Page 51: The Flying Seagull Project

Page 56: Jerry Monkman/Ecophotography

Page 57: Nadezhda1906, Getty Images/Istockphoto

Page 58: Igor Stevanovich, Getty Images/Istockphoto

Page 62: William Howard, Getty Images/Istockphoto

Page 124: Benardo Bodo, Getty Images/Istockphoto

Page 126: Liudmyla Supynska, Getty Images/Istockphoto

Page 129: Dari Streater

Page 131: Last 19, Getty Images/Istockphoto

Page 134: Delaney Streater

Page 137: Dawson Streater

Page 139: Moto

Page 142: Redmond Rotary Club

Page 144: Julie Martin

Page 147: John Ferraro

CPSIA information can be obtained
at www.ICGtesting.com
Printed in the USA
LVHW051020231220
674967LV00008B/193